ALEXANDER FLEMING

Makers of Modern Science

ALEXANDER FLEMING
Conquering Disease with Penicillin

Steven Otfinoski

Facts On File
New York • Oxford

ALEXANDER FLEMING: Conquering Disease with Penicillin

Facts On File, Inc.
460 Park Avenue South
New York NY 10016
USA

Facts On File Limited
c/o Roundhouse Publishing Ltd.
P.O. Box 140
Oxford OX2 7SF
United Kingdom

Library of Congress Cataloging-in-Publication Data
Otfinoski, Steven
    Alexander Fleming : conquering disease with penicillin / Steven Otfinoski
        p. cm. — (Makers of modern science)
    Includes bibliographical references (p.) and index.
    Summary: Describes the life of Alexander Fleming and his work in using penicillin to conquer diseases.
        ISBN 0-8160-2752-8 (acid-free paper)
        1. Fleming, Alexander, 1881–1955—Juvenile literature.
    2. Bacteriologists—Great Britain—Biography—Juvenile literature.
    3. Penicillin—History—Juvenile literature. [1. Fleming,
    Alexander, 1881–1955. 2. Scientists. 3. Penicillin—History.]
    I. Title. II. Series.
    QR31.F5073 1993
    616'.014'092—dc20   92-9910
    [B]

A British CIP catalogue record for this book is available from the British Library.

Facts On File books are available at special discounts when purchased in bulk quantities for businesses, associations, institutions or sales promotions. Please contact our Special Sales Department in New York at 212/683-2244 (dial 800/322-8755 except in NY, AK or HI) or in Oxford at 865/728399.

Text design by Ron Monteleone
Jacket design by Catherine Hyman
Composition by Facts On File, Inc./Grace M. Ferrara
Manufactured by R.R. Donnelley & Sons
Printed in the United States of America

10 9 8 7 6 5 4 3 2 1

This book is printed on acid-free paper.

To Beverly,
who shared the adventure

CONTENTS

ACKNOWLEDGMENTS

The author would like to thank Charlie Woodward of the Kilmarnock and Loudoun District Libraries of the Dick Institute, Kilmarnock, Scotland for his assistance in researching this biography.

INTRODUCTION

My search for Alexander Fleming began in Kilmarnock, a large town in the southwest Scottish county of Ayr. As a boy, Fleming had gone to school in Kilmarnock. I started my quest at the local library, an impressive building surrounded by colorful flower beds. The helpful Kilmarnock librarian put together a street-by-street map for me of the nearby village of Darvel, pinpointing Lochfield, the farm where Fleming spent his earliest years.

Accompanied by my wife and mother, I drove the 10 miles or so in our rented car to Darvel. There we found a small square in the center of the modest town where a bust of Darvel's most famous son sat on a pedestal. Across the street was the local library, small compared to Kilmarnock's, but where I hoped to find more personal information on Fleming.

Unfortunately, there were only five minutes left until closing, and I barely had time to introduce myself to the smiling girl behind the desk, grab some pamphlets and take a quick snapshot of a splendid portrait of Fleming hanging on the wall behind the circulation desk. (It came out overexposed.)

Then, armed with our maps, the Otfinoskis followed the twisting country lane to Lochfield. The farm proved far easier to locate on the map than in the sea of grassy moorlands surrounding us. After 20 minutes of futile searching, we pulled into the dirt driveway of a simple stone farmhouse and inquired of the lady of the house where Lochfield was. Regarding me and my American accent as about as alien as a visitor from outer space, the woman pointed into the distance and in her soft Scottish burr gave me directions.

Ten minutes later, down progressively rockier roads we drove. Finally, on a worn, wooden fence, against a huge meadow studded with grazing cows, was a yellow sign reading LOCHFIELD. The only house in sight, however, lay in the far distance. To make matters

This impressive granite monument to one of the 20th century's greatest medical scientists was first unveiled at Lochfield in 1957, two years after Fleming's death. (author's photo)

worse, the rusty iron gate on the road to the house was securely closed. Somewhat guiltily I undid the gate and we drove up the winding dirt road to—another gate. All in all, we passed through four gates before we finally came in sight again of the farmhouse. The road became increasingly stony and rutted, as our car's shock absorbers would attest.

As we drove the final quarter mile, I mentally composed what I was going to say to the present owners, who might not be overjoyed to see three Yanks trespassing on their property. I need not have bothered. The house—a sturdy whitewashed stone farmhouse—was deserted and in disrepair. However, on closer inspection, there were signs of renovation—a wheelbarrow here, a pile of wood there. Whoever was planning to move back into Lochfield wasn't around, much to my relief.

There, by a stone shed, near the corner of the house, was a craggy, granite monument, over five feet high. Chiseled into the speckled, shiny red surface of the stone were these words:

> SIR ALEXANDER FLEMING
> DISCOVER OF PENICILLIN
> WAS BORN HERE AT LOCHFIELD
> ON 6TH AUGUST 1881.

Simple. Terse. To the point. Much like the man himself. The distance from the granite marker to the farmhouse was only a few feet, but the distance Fleming traveled from this humble beginning to the heights of fame and greatness as a scientist was a long way indeed.

After snapping a few more pictures, we left Lochfield to the bleating sheep and the blowing wind. I shut each gate carefully behind us, so no cows or sheep would wander away in our wake. And as I stole one last look at the forlorn farmhouse, I could only wonder how such a stark, lonely place could have produced one of our century's greatest scientists.

1

THE MAGICAL MOLD

For the birth of something new, there has to be a happening. Newton saw an apple fall; James Watt watched a kettle boil; Roentgen fogged some photographic plates. And these people knew enough to translate ordinary happenings into something new . . .

—Alexander Fleming

The truth is, if Alexander Fleming had been a tidy man, he might have never made the greatest medical discovery of the 20th century. Not that Fleming was a sloppy scientist. Far from it; he was a meticulous worker, carrying out each experiment with methodical thoroughness. But he was a "hands-on" bacteriologist and he liked to have all his apparatus within easy reach. So he kept his little glass plates and shallow, round Petri dishes piled high on his workbench. To a visitor his little laboratory in the inoculation department of London's St. Mary's Medical School might have looked like random disorder, but Fleming knew better.

What people thought didn't bother Fleming. At 47, the dour little Scotsman had proven himself to be a bacteriologist of some note. He had done valuable research on bacteria—the tiny organisms that cause disease and infection. He had served his country in World War I, written a score or more of noteworthy scientific papers, and even discovered a natural germ-killing substance in living things. Unfortunately, he had run into difficulties purifying the substance so it could be of practical use, and the medical community had taken scant notice. But then Fleming, while an innovative and hardworking scientist, lacked the gift for self-promotion that brings fame and glory.

Now in middle age, Alexander Fleming looked forward to another 20 years or so of meaningful work in his dingy lab on Praed Street in Paddington. Then he contemplated a pleasant retirement filled with fishing, gardening, and golf. It was not a bad future. He had hoped for more, but he was content. He had a loving wife and son, a home in the city, and a house in the country where he could escape on weekends. Life was good, if not terribly exciting.

That summer of 1928 had been a damp and humid one. The stale air in his tiny room and the dull routine of his research might have made another man irritable and crabby. But Fleming had an even temper, and he enjoyed company. His door was always open and colleagues dropped in regularly to see what old "Flem" was up to.

At the moment he was busy writing an article on the bacterium *Staphylococci,* a long name for a nasty germ that caused boils and other illnesses. The article was to be included in a massive work, *A System of Bacteriology,* to be published by the Medical Research Council.

Fleming had been experimenting with the germ; glass dishes of the cultured bacteria cluttered his workbench amid crumpled, empty cigarette packs. Other researchers routinely tossed out their cultures as soon as they were through with them, but Flem had a funny habit of leaving them laying around for a week or so. Then he would look over each dish to see if there were any interesting changes in the bacteria. Whatever he hoped to find in a week-old Petri dish was anyone's guess.

On this particular September afternoon, Merlin Pryce, a colleague, wandered through the open door and started to chat with the older man. Fleming, like many Scots, had a keen aversion to small talk. But his colleagues had accepted his silences and knew that beneath his often stony exterior there beat a warm, kind heart.

As the two men talked, Fleming absentmindedly looked at the collected culture dishes on his bench. Suddenly he stopped talking, looked curiously at one dish, and muttered half to himself, "That's funny . . . " Pryce stared at the dish in Fleming's hand. There was a bluish mold growing on it. This was nothing extraordinary. Molds, a kind of fungi, will grow on almost any living host, and a colony of bacteria looks as good a home for it as any stale piece of bread. Tiny mold spores had undoubtedly floated in from outside, landed on the uncovered dish, and sprouted into a colony.

This was a process both men had seen a hundred times before. What Fleming's keen blue eyes noted, however, was the unusual effect the mold had on the yellow colonies of bacteria in the dish. All around the mold were clear rings where the bacteria should have been growing. The culture had dissolved wherever it came in contact with the mold. Something in the mold was clearly killing the microbes.

Pryce wasn't terribly impressed. The fact that the mold contained some substance that killed a few germs was curious, but of no special importance. Yet for Fleming it was something worth following up on. "Instead of casting out the contaminated culture, with appropriate language, I made some investigations," he later wrote.

He scraped a tiny piece of the blue mold from the dish and examined it under his microscope. Although Fleming was no mold expert, he recognized the brushlike hairs as characteristic of a mold of the genus *Penicillium*—one of the commonest of molds.

Fleming's curiosity was now thoroughly aroused. He removed the rest of the mold from the dish and put it in a jar of broth, a nutritive soup in which organisms can grow and be observed. Within a matter of days the mold had grown into a complicated colony on the surface of the broth. This white "scum" soon turned green and eventually black. But what was most extraordinary was that the mold had turned the clear liquid beneath it a bright yellow. Fleming deduced that the mold was releasing the bacteria-killing agent into the broth, giving it its golden hue. Furthermore, when he tested the liquid on cultures of bacteria, it proved as effective a killer as the mold itself.

Did other molds have the same effect on germs? He set about to find out. Fleming collected molds wherever he could find them, even on the old shoes of friends. He tested each mold and found none contained the germ-killing substance found in the *Penicillium* mold. Fleming was hooked. He put aside all other work and devoted his working hours to studying this magical mold and its golden juice.

Alexander Fleming exhibits the bacteria-killing penicillin mold he discovered years earlier in this same tiny laboratory at St. Mary's Hospital. Note the stacks of Petri dishes and other paraphernalia. (UPI/Bettmann)

Soon he had transformed his tiny lab into a breeding ground for molds. He put some of the broth into trenches on a plate of agar—a gelatinlike extract of seaweed in which cultures of bacteria could grow and be studied. Then he introduced different microbes to the plate to see what would happen. The broth soaked through the agar and stopped the germ colonies from growing. In a few days Fleming noticed that not only were the *Staphylococcus* microbes dead but so were several other kinds of germs on the plate. Further experiments showed the mold juice to be an immensely powerful germ killer. When Fleming diluted it to 1,000th of its original strength in water, it still retained its germ-killing ability.

Fleming shared his findings with his fellow researcher, Stuart Craddock. "Take a look at that, it's interesting—the kind of thing I like; it may well turn out to be important," he told Craddock, showing him the mold juice. Craddock examined it and showed polite interest, little more. Fleming knew it would take more evidence to convince his colleague he was on to something extraordinary.

Craddock had been working with Fleming on a chemical called mercuric chloride. It proved to be an effective germ killer, but unfortunately, it also killed the very cells it was supposed to be protecting. Would the mold juice Fleming was testing also prove toxic to living tissue?

Fleming injected the juice into a rabbit and a mouse. The next morning both patients were alive and well. Craddock was impressed. The two took the mold to St. Mary's resident mold expert, Professor J. C. La Touche, affectionately known to the staff as "Old Moldy." La Touche identified the mold more precisely as *Penicillium rubrum* and supported the theory that it probably drifted in from Praed Street through the window.*

"There are thousands of different molds and there were thousands of different bacteria," Fleming noted years later, "and that chance put that mold in the right spot at the right time was like winning the Irish Sweep."

The wondrous substance in the mold juice that killed germs had to be given a name. No fancy scientific nomenclature would do, Fleming decided. The name of this magical drug should pay homage to its humble parent—a common mold similar to the one found in a week-old piece of cheese. He shortened the mold's name and called his discovery penicillin.

---

* Fleming biographer Gwyn Macfarlane gives convincing evidence that the famous mold spore probably came into Fleming's laboratory not through the window, as generally believed, but through the door. It most likely drifted in from La Touche's own lab, which was directly below Fleming's.

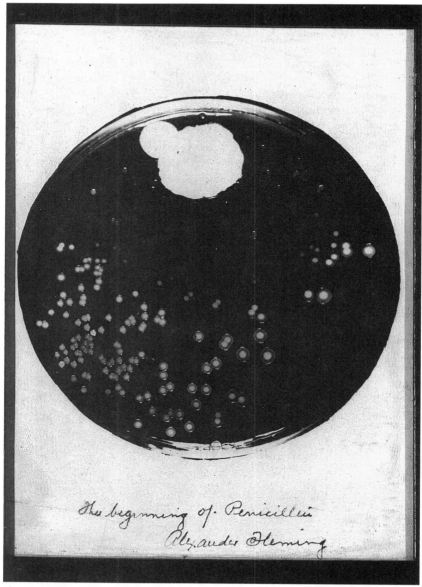

The beginning of Penicillin

Alexander Fleming

Fleming himself took this photograph of his original penicillin plate. Note how the colonies of staphylococal germs have disappeared around the mold—the large white area to the left. (UPI/Bettmann)

CHAPTER 1 NOTES

p. 1   "For the birth of something new . . ." André Maurois, *The Life of Sir Alexander Fleming,* p. 167.

p. 3   "Instead of casting out . . ." John Rowland, *The Penicillin Man: The Story of Sir Alexander Fleming,* p. 93.

p. 4   "Take a look at that . . ." Maurois, *The Life of Sir Alexander Fleming,* p. 125.

2

AN AYRSHIRE BOYHOOD

That young Fleming, that young Fleming will get
somewhere before he's many years older.

—Marion Stirling, one of Fleming's first teachers

The Flemings probably immigrated to the Scottish Lowlands from western Belgium several hundred years earlier. The people of that region of Belgium are Flemish, hence the family name. The Flemings brought two professions with them from their native land— weaving and farming. It was as a farmer that Hugh Fleming, Alexander's grandfather, made his mark in the Lowlands in the early 1800s. His son, Hugh II, established the family farm at Lochfield. Like many poor Scots, Hugh couldn't afford to own his own farm. Instead he rented the land and farmhouse from the absent owner, the earl of Loudoun.

Lowlands is something of a misnomer, for Lochfield lay at an altitude of 800 feet. The soil was stony and shallow, the climate cold and damp. The Flemings eked out a meager living raising sheep, growing oats, and selling eggs and butter on their 800 acres of moorland.

It was a hard life. Hugh's first wife, Jane, died of tuberculosis after the birth of their fourth child. At age 60, he married a young, energetic woman, Grace Morton. They had four more children together—Grace, John, Alexander (whom everyone called Alec), and Robert.

The Flemings may have been relatively poor in material things, but they were rich in the world of nature that surrounded them. While their older half-brothers and sisters took care of the heavy farm chores, the young Fleming boys were free to spend much of their time exploring the wild valleys and moors surrounding their home. They stole bird's eggs to sell to traveling salesmen, snared rabbits, caught trout in rushing streams with their bare hands (a sport known as guddling) and in the winter rode peat carts for toboggans. The family used peat, the thick sod of the moors, as fuel for heating and cooking. "As boys we had many advantages over the boys living in the towns," Fleming later recalled. "We automatically learned many things that they missed, and it was just the chance of living away from people which taught us those things."

The world of Lochfield nurtured a love of nature and its creatures that Alec Fleming would carry with him throughout his life. Equally important, it developed in the boy keen powers of observation that would later play a critical role in his greatest scientific discoveries.

In 1887 when Alec was seven, Hugh Fleming died from a stroke. Alec remembered his father fondly but somewhat distantly as an old man sitting by the fire. Mother Grace took over the running of

The simple stone farmhouse at Lochfield in Ayrshire, Scotland where Fleming spent his childhood is still a working farm today. (author's photo)

the farm, with the strong support of her eldest stepson, Hugh III. As in many traditional farming cultures, the eldest son was destined to take over the farm from his father. Soon after, the earl of Loudoun declared Hugh the new tenant of Lochfield.

Independent until 1746, when their country was incorporated into Great Britain, the Scots are a proud people who place a high importance on education. Many younger sons, finding few opportunities at home, go off to university and then south to London, Britain's capital, to seek their fortune. This is the route Alec's older brothers took and one he himself would later follow.

At the age of five, Alec entered what the Scots call a "wee" school in the tiny village of Loudon Moor. The one-room schoolhouse was a modest one, heated by the peat the schoolchildren brought from home. In the winter, Alec's mother would sometimes put two hot potatoes in his pockets to keep his hands warm on the long walk to school. Later, he ate them for lunch. Modest though the school might have been, the teachers took their charge seriously. Fleming fondly recalled spending "the brightest part of my schooldays" there.

Many years later, when Fleming had become a world-famous figure, he would receive a letter from one of his favorite Loudon Moor teachers, Marion Stirling. "This little letter is just to congratulate my dear little friend of many moons ago . . ." she wrote. "By the way, your wonderful injections [of penicillin] cured a very delicate little grand-niece of mine . . ." It was a letter Fleming cherished above many from more distinguished writers.

Young Alec was short but athletically built, fair-haired, with a wide forehead, penetrating blue eyes, and a shy but winning smile. "He was always thinking something up," his younger brother Robert later wrote, "but if it didn't work, he lost no time in modifying it or discarding it altogether and thinking up something else." Learning was never a chore for Alec Fleming. He enjoyed it as he would any challenging game.

At age 10, Alec moved on to the bigger school at Darvel. He continued to do well but missed the personal attention given at Loudon Moor. The most memorable event in his two years at Darvel was an unfortunate accident. One day Alec was racing around a corner when he ran headfirst into another student. His nose was broken in the collision, flattening it for life. This later gave rise to the unfounded rumor that the discoverer of penicillin had, in his younger days, been a professional prizefighter.

The Fleming family was impressed enough with Alec's academic progress to send him to the prestigious Kilmarnock Academy. The school was 16 miles away, and Alec had to live apart from his family for the first time. He returned home to Lochfield on weekends by train. The classes at the academy were large and somewhat impersonal. "Not much chance of individual attention," Fleming later wrote. "But we worked well."

At 14, Alec felt he had learned everything he could at the academy. The larger world beckoned. Two of his older brothers and one sister were already living and working in London. Tom had become an eye doctor, or "oculist," prescribing spectacles for patients. John became apprenticed to a lenses-manufacturing company, and Mary kept house for both of them. At their invitation, Alec joined them in a house Tom had bought on respectable York Street.

London in 1895 was one of the most exciting cities on earth. The British Empire was at its peak, and its capital city was a thriving center of industry, commerce, and the arts. It must have been a bit overwhelming for a young Scottish farm lad.

Alec soon signed up for courses at the Polytechnic Institute in Regent Street where he studied alongside his younger brother Robert, who joined the family in London six months later. Alec's Scottish education put him so far ahead of his fellow students that he moved up four classes in just two weeks. Excelling in every course he took, Alec left the Polytechnic Institute at age 16. Although he no longer found the school challenging, the larger reason for his leaving was economic. Tom Fleming was straining to pay for his brother's education, and Alec felt guilty about this. He decided it was time to go to work and start paying his share of the bills.

Having no particular interest in any profession, Alec took a job as a junior clerk in the office of a shipping company for 10 shillings a week. His days were spent sitting on a tall stool in a back room, where he wrote down cargo lists of goods arriving in London into a huge, dusty ledger. For a young man of ability and intellect, it was deadly boring work.

To escape the drudgery of his job, Alec joined an organization that would remain dear to his heart all his life—the London Scottish Volunteers. This group of part-time soldiers was founded in the early 1800s to help defend the nation against Napoleon's army. The Scottish Volunteers, with their bright kilts and droning bagpipes, were a proud outfit that gave dislocated Scots a way to meet fellow countrymen and keep their rich heritage alive.

In 1900 the Boer War against South Africa broke out, but few of the Scottish Volunteers were sent to fight. The only action most of them saw was on weekend maneuvers and summer camp. Alec joined the rifle team; his sharp eye made him a crack shot. He won prizes and trophies at more than one shooting match. He was also an excellent swimmer and joined the regiment's water polo team. One of the teams they played against was from St. Mary's Hospital in the Paddington section of London.

As a young man, Alec Fleming was an interesting study in contrasts. Quiet, saying little unless he had something important to say, he had few close friends outside the family circle. On the other hand, he loved the comradeship of the volunteers, enjoying the games and fun of barracks life. Curiously, he had no ambition to be an officer and was content to remain a private throughout his years in the volunteers.

On the job, Alec was an exemplary worker. Despite the monotony, he might have stayed on in the shipping office for years, but in 1901, at age 20, an unexpected event changed his life forever. A bachelor uncle, John Fleming, who was a prosperous farmer, died and left a substantial legacy to his relatives. Alec's share of the money was £250—a considerable sum in those days.

He wanted to use the bequest to get started in a career. But what career to chose? His brother Thomas, now a successful eye doctor, urged him to follow in his footsteps and pursue medicine. This seemed a logical choice, since two of his other brothers were doing quite well in the profession and two of his sisters had married doctors. So Alec set his course for medicine, despite the fact that he felt no burning desire to be a doctor.

He was a bit old to be starting medical school and had to first pass a matriculation equivalency exam in order to apply. Alec amazed everyone by taking top honors in Great Britain on the test after only a few lessons in medicine.

He now had to choose a medical school. There were 12 in London and several in the vicinity of where the Flemings lived. It was then that Alec remembered the water polo match against the team from St. Mary's. He recalled it was a team he wouldn't have minded playing on himself. For this most whimsical of reasons, young Alexander Fleming applied to and was accepted at St. Mary's Hospital Medical School.

CHAPTER 2 NOTES

p. 9   "That young Fleming . . ." John Rowland, *The Penicillin Man*, pp. 13–14.

p. 10   "As boys we had many advantages . . ." L. J. Ludovici, *Fleming: Discoverer of Penicillin*, p. 22.

p. 11   "This little letter . . ." André Maurois, *The Life of Sir Alexander Fleming*, p. 210.

p. 11   "He was always thinking . . ." Ludovici, *Fleming*, p. 23.

3

MEDICINE AND MARKSMANSHIP

There is no better way to learn about human nature than by indulging in sports, more especially in team-sports.

—Alexander Fleming

The teaching hospital that Alec Fleming had chosen to attend was the newest in London, having been founded in 1845. However, its facilities were little better than its centuries-old rivals. Unlike today's gleaming white hospital wards, St. Mary's was dark, drafty, and dirty. Furthermore, the hospital was in serious financial trouble, having overextended itself for several years. None of this daunted young Fleming and the other 79 members of the class of 1901. For although their surroundings may have been old-fashioned, the field of medicine itself was entering a new and exciting age.

Thanks to such giants as Louis Pasteur in France, Edward Jenner and Joseph Lister in England, and Robert Koch in Germany, medical science had made dramatic advances in the last half of the 19th century. The dream of ending the scourge of disease and prolonging human life far beyond what most people thought possible now seemed within grasp. Pasteur, perhaps the greatest man of medicine of the 19th century, first proposed the revolutionary theory that disease was caused by microscopic single-celled organisms called bacteria.

Bacteria are the oldest and most numerous forms of life on earth. They are also among the smallest and fastest-growing organisms known. One spoonful of earth can contain over a billion of them. Although there are more than 2,500 kinds of bacteria, the vast majority of them are harmless to humans. In fact, some are actually beneficial, helping to aid digestion and producing vitamins in the human body. But other bacteria can attack and feed on living tissue, causing infection and disease.

A second major source of infection are viruses. Viruses are far smaller than even bacteria. The largest virus is about one-tenth the size of an average bacterium. Influenza, measles, rabies, and even the common cold are all caused by viruses. AIDS, the most dreaded disease of our age, is caused by HIV (human immunodeficiency virus), which attacks the human immune system.

Unlike bacteria, a virus is so primitive that it is not made up of cells, but consists of a core of a nucleic acid and an outer coat of protein. To thrive and multiply, viruses must invade the cells of other living things. Once they are carried into human, animal, and plant bodies by wind or other means, they live and grow off the living cells, usually killing them in the process. Disease-causing viruses and bacteria are often simply called germs or microbes.

English doctor Edward Jenner (1749–1823) came to the extraordinary conclusion that weakened bacteria and viruses that cause specific diseases could be injected into a patient in minute amounts with beneficial results. Instead of causing the person to contract the disease, the germs could actually *prevent* the patient from getting the disease in the future. Jenner demonstrated that this process—now known as inoculation or vaccination—could stir up natural substances in the blood known as antibodies and cause them to attack and destroy the invading germs. The antibodies retained the "memory" of the attack and remained on guard against the first signs of another invasion. Jenner proved his theory by developing a successful serum, or vaccine, against the deadly disease of smallpox, from the pus of cowpox, a related disease. In 1796 he injected an eight-year-old boy with this serum and made him immune to smallpox.

Other medical scientists, most prominently Pasteur in France, followed Jenner's lead. Pasteur developed a vaccine against rabies, a disease caused by a virus spread from the bite of sick animals.

Robert Koch's work in Germany led to a whole new branch of medical science—bacteriology, the study of bacteria in the human body. In the 1870s and 1880s, he discovered the agents in bacteria that caused such dreaded diseases as anthrax, tuberculosis, and cholera. He went on to prove that bubonic plague was spread by bacteria-ridden fleas.

Pasteur and Koch raised an issue that by Fleming's day had become a major debate among medical scientists. Is the best defense against disease the body's own natural defense system or artificial chemicals? Jenner, Pasteur, and Koch seemed to make the case for the body's immune system. Joseph Lister, a leading surgeon who pioneered the use of powerful germ-killing chemicals, called antiseptics, championed artificial means.

In the midst of this debate entered an English doctor who would put St. Mary's on the cutting edge of medical science. His name was Sir Almroth Wright. In 1898 Wright became the first doctor to use a killed vaccine on humans to fight and prevent the disease typhoid. Alexander Fleming, years later, pointed out the significance of Wright's achievement:

> *Pasteur had once and for all established the principle of prophylactic [preventive] inoculation against infective disease, but he had used* living *vaccines in his work. This was possible in treating animals but it was not, owing to certain risks, suitable for the treatment of humans. The introduction of* killed *vaccines for the prevention and treatment of disease was largely the work of our great countryman, Sir Almroth Wright.*

Despite this success, Wright's fight to make immunization compulsory in the English army met with staunch resistance. Army officials, along with many physicians of the day, were still skeptical of the newfangled theory of inoculation.

Frustrated, Wright quit his job with the army and took a position at St. Mary's, where he became professor of pathology the year after Fleming entered the medical school. Pathology was another new branch of medicine that dealt with the nature of disease. Under Wright's domineering personality, the inoculation department at St. Mary's would play a central role in the struggle against disease.

The admiration and devotion that Wright inspired in his students and co-workers was due as much to his charismatic personality as it was to his medical gifts. Physically he was an imposing figure—a bear of a man with huge, expressive eyebrows that a former student claimed he "could almost speak with." Wright was a truly Renaissance man whose interests ranged far beyond the laboratory. He claimed to have memorized 250,000 lines of poetry and spouted off a few favorite lines whenever the occasion warranted it. He was also a gifted writer and a master linguist who learned an Eskimo language when he was over 80. His friends were the great and famous of his day. The playwright George Bernard Shaw was a close crony who often dropped by the lab for a chat or to watch Wright at work. Shaw even used Wright as the model for the leading character in his play *The Doctor's Dilemma.*

But Wright's outspokenness also made him many enemies in the medical world. He held strong opinions on nearly every subject, from bacteriology to women's rights, which he flatly opposed. The fierce debate between those in favor of seeking ways to aid and support the body's natural defenses and those in favor of chemical germ killers was one he reveled in.

While Wright was becoming the shining star of St. Mary's faculty, Alec Fleming, in his more quiet way, was building a reputation as a model student. He won the hospital's entrance scholarship, which paid all his tuition fees in his first year there. In his second year, he won both the Anatomy Prize and the Physiology Prize.

The amazing thing about Fleming's academic career was not how hard he worked at his studies but how little time he put in on the books. "He never burdened himself with unnecessary work," explained fellow student and lifelong friend Professor Charles Pannett, "but would pick out from his text-books just what he needed, and neglect the rest."

Fleming's success stemmed from an incredible memory, a talent for cutting through to the essence of a subject, and an uncanny ability to do well on tests. "I felt he could gauge the slant of examiners' minds in some astonishing way, even to the point of anticipating just the sort of questions they were going to ask him!" Pannett recalled.

St. Mary's Teaching Hospital of London, founded in 1845, as it looked in 1977. Fleming attended medical school here and stayed on as a bacteriologist for the rest of his career. The laboratory where he discovered penicillin is on this facade, facing Praed Street. (Bettmann/Hulton)

Like Wright, Fleming's interests were not confined to the classroom. He joined the water polo team he once competed against as well as the swimming team and the rifle team. Fleming would come to see sports not as a release from study, but as an integral part of his education. "When you are one of a team, you have to play for the side and not simply for yourself," he later wrote, "and this is marvelous training for a man who hopes to become a doctor. For even a doctor has to play the game of life, not just for his own material advantage, but for the welfare of his patients, irrespective of financial gain."

There was certainly little financial gain to be had from being a bacteriologist. Nor was it a glamorous profession. Bacteriologists were primarily research workers, studying different bacteria, conducting endless experiments on them, and dutifully noting the results. It is not surprising that despite his admiration for Wright as a teacher, Fleming was not immediately drawn to follow in his footsteps.

Surgery was the area of most interest to Fleming. The surgeon then, as today, was seen as the prince of the medical profession. With his steady eye and deft hands, Fleming knew he could be as good a surgeon as he was a marksman.

The medical school's curriculum was split into two parts—the preclinical and clinical courses. In the first half, students learned the basics of biology, chemistry, and physics in the classroom. In the second half, they worked in the hospital gaining practical experience. They trained under a senior clinician and worked in the outpatient department, doing everything from stitching cuts to extracting teeth.

In June 1905 Fleming passed the primary exam for the Fellowship of the Royal College of Surgeons. His field of choice was obstetrics, the delivery of babies, and he spent a month attending to maternity cases outside the hospital.

A year and a half later he passed his final exams and qualified as a doctor. Two choices lay ahead of him now. He could go straight into general practice in London, or he could apply for a hospital appointment at St. Mary's or another institution. He did neither. The decision he made was once again determined not by career considerations but by sports.

On Almroth Wright's staff in the inoculation department there was a good-humored young doctor named John Freeman. Like Fleming, Freeman had a passion for shooting. He knew Fleming was a crack shot. With him on their rifle team, Freeman thought St. Mary's had a good chance of winning the prestigious Armitage Cup. But to keep Fleming on the team, Freeman had to find a way to keep him at St. Mary's. He remembered there was a vacancy for a junior assistant on Wright's staff.

"I plugged the fact that Almroth Wright's lab would make a good observation-post from which he [Fleming] could keep an eye open for a chance to get into surgery," Freeman later explained. "I told him, too, that he would find work in the lab interesting, and that the company there was congenial."

Freeman was obviously a persuasive salesman, for in the summer of 1906, on his 25th birthday, Fleming joined Wright's staff in the inoculation department. Much to his surprise, Fleming indeed found the work interesting—so interesting that he never left.

CHAPTER 3 NOTES

p. 15   "There is no better way . . ." André Maurois, *The Life of Sir Alexander Fleming,* p. 37.

p. 17   "Pasteur had once . . ." L. J. Ludovici, *Fleming: Discoverer of Penicillin,* p. 12.

p. 18   "He never burdened himself . . ." Maurois, *The Life of Sir Alexander Fleming,* p. 31.

p. 18   "I felt he could gauge . . ." Ludovici, *Fleming,* p. 32.

p. 20   "When you are one of a team . . ." Maurois, *The Life of Sir Alexander Fleming,* pp. 37–38.

p. 21   "I plugged the fact . . ." Maurois, *The Life of Sir Alexander Fleming,* p. 37.

4

WORKING FOR THE "OLD MAN"

Of all the evils which befall man in his civilized state, the evil of disease is incomparably the greatest . . .

> —Almroth Wright in his article "The World's Greatest Problem"

It might have been marksmanship that brought Alexander Fleming to Almroth Wright's inoculation department, but it was a newfound love of bacterial research that kept him there. As a medical student, Fleming had always been fascinated with problem solving—not content with observing a change in the world of the laboratory, but wanting to know why it took place. It was this love of knowledge for its own sake and the urgency of Wright's mission that eventually turned Fleming from the operating room toward the laboratory.

Like most major decisions people make in life, this wasn't a sudden one. In 1908, after more than a year in Wright's lab, Fleming was still interested enough in surgery to take a job working part time as a house surgeon, performing minor operations and assisting at major ones.

The following June he took his final surgeon's exam. He later jokingly attributed this decision to his thrifty nature. "Being a Scot," he wrote, "I never ceased to regret the five pounds which I had spent to no purpose [on the first exam for surgeons]. I wondered whether I ought not, perhaps, to have a shot at the final." He passed with flying colors and became a member of the

Fellowship of the Royal College of Surgeons, although he never performed another operation.

Certainly, Almroth Wright had a lot to do with Fleming's decision to become a bacteriologist. Wright's work at St. Mary's in finding new ways to support the body's immune system was of world importance, and his enthusiasm caught on like wildfire among his disciples in the inoculation department.

When Fleming came aboard, Wright's work was centered on the most important player in the human immune system—white blood cells. Blood contains many different cells and substances. The most numerous of these are red blood cells, which carry out the exchange of oxygen and carbon dioxide between the lungs and body tissues. White blood cells, also called leukocytes, defend the body against bacteria and other infecting organisms. In the presence of an infection, the white cells multiply dramatically, overwhelming and swallowing the invading bacteria. The specific white cells that perform this important function are called phagocytes. They were named by the Russian-French bacteriologist Elie Metchnikoff, who first observed their behavior in 1882.

At St. Mary's, Wright explored the process of phagocytosis— where phagocytes engulf and "eat" microbes—with startling results. He placed a drop of blood on a glass slide and introduced microbes to stimulate the phagocytes. When the blood dried, he studied it under a microscope and could actually count the microbes inside each white blood cell. By comparing the average number of "eaten" microbes with the normal number of microbes in a cell, Wright reached what he called the phagocytic index for that particular blood sample.

He then discovered a substance in the clear liquid part of blood called serum that made the microbes more "appetizing" to the phagocytes. A lover of classical Greek, Wright called the new substance opsonin, which means "I prepare food" in Greek. He coated microbes with opsonin in a serum and then offered them to some phagocytes. The white cells ate more microbes than they had under normal conditions. By comparing this microbe count with that of unprepared microbes, Wright arrived at what he called the opsonic index.

A vaccination with opsonin-coated microbes would, Wright proved, greatly increase the efficiency of the phagocytes and more effectively prevent disease. By knowing a patient's opsonic index, Wright could also determine the best treatment—by either raising or lowering the index with more opsonin. In his play *The Doctor's Dilemma,* Shaw humorously referred to opsonin as "what you butter the disease germs with to make your white blood corpuscles eat them."

Determining the opsonic index in blood samples from different patients was the tedious task set before Fleming and Wright's other assistants. They worked up to 16 hours a day preparing blood slides and counting microbes. At the end of their long day in the lab, they often adjourned to a room called the library (although it contained no books), where Wright would hold court. During these ritual "midnight teas" the research assistants would eat, drink, and listen to Wright discourse on whatever topic took his fancy.

Wright took a perverse pleasure in intimidating his staff at such times. One of his favorite ploys was to quote a few lines of poetry from his encyclopedic memory and then turn on an unwary assistant and challenge him to give the source. Fleming, the ever-observant student, noted over time that Wright most often quoted from Milton's epic poem "Paradise Lost." He realized that if he named the poem whenever Wright called on him, he had one chance in three of being right.

The teas often lasted till two or three in the morning, after which the bone-weary staff caught a few hours' sleep before returning to the lab to begin another day's work. Fleming thrived on this grinding schedule, and in a 1909 issue of a hospital publication he was referred to as "one of Sir Almroth Wright's most enthusiastic followers."

Despite his enthusiasm for his boss, "Little Flem," as his colleagues fondly called him, was anything but a blind follower. When Wright, who placed a great stock in his intuitive powers, built up an elaborate theory which the others listened to in uncritical silence, Fleming would reply softly but firmly, "It won't work, Chief."

There was no pride or vanity in Fleming's statement. He simply knew he was right and said so. "People don't usually like those

Sir Almroth Wright, Fleming's teacher, mentor, and boss at St. Mary's inoculation department, is seen here in a characteristically intimidating pose in his London study. (Bettmann/Hulton)

who are always right," admitted a colleague, Dr. R. M. Fry, years later. "But he [Fleming] was so nice about it, that you couldn't not like him. Of course, he couldn't resist saying 'I told you so,' but he said it as a child might have done. He loved pulling your leg if he had done something better than you, and enjoyed it all thoroughly. By great good luck, there were very few in the lab who hadn't got a sense of humor. No one without it would have lasted long with Wright and Fleming always ready to poke fun at them, each in his own way."

Not everyone, however, appreciated Wright's humor, nor his achievements. He had as many enemies as he had followers and friends. If he was called affectionately the "Old Man" by his assistants and students, he was "Sir Almost Right" to his critics. Wright's highly individualistic and dogmatic approach to science only made him an easier target for his detractors.

"The time when the doctor will be, for the most part, an immunizer is visibly drawing nearer," he once claimed. Another time he boasted, "One experiment suffices, properly performed, to establish the truth of a principle." Such wrongheaded predictions and sweeping generalizations would not be a part of Fleming's future scientific method. Like his colleagues, he may have idolized Wright, but he would not imitate him.

In May 1908 Fleming published his first solo scientific paper in the medical journal *The Practitioner.* It was entitled "Some Observations on the Opsonic Index with Special Reference to the Accuracy of the Method and to Some Like Sources of Error." The title may have been daunting, but the paper itself was written clearly and simply. Fleming's writing style was less formidable and more imaginative than that of most of his contemporaries—dry professionals writing for an audience of dry professionals. In a later paper, for instance, Fleming compared test tubes to a "company of soldiers, drawn up in two ranks, each rear rank tube covering one of the front rank."

Further evidence of the artistic side of Fleming's personality was brought out in his friendship with the artist Ronald Gray. Gray, who had a tubercular knee, was recommended to Fleming by a mutual friend. He prescribed a series of vaccine injections and plenty of exercise. The knee was cured and the grateful painter became fast friends with the unassuming Scotsman.

Fleming enjoyed Gray's company and that of his artist friends, and soon Gray nominated him for membership in the prestigious Chelsea Arts Club. To become a member, however, Fleming was required to submit a finished picture to show he was a bona fide artist. Gray, a staunch traditionalist, saw this as an opportunity to have some fun with the "modern art" movement that was beginning to infiltrate England from abroad.

Fleming, who enjoyed a good joke, went along with the hoax and painted a picture in the "modern style." Biographers disagree as to what exactly was the subject of Fleming's first canvas. In his biography of Fleming, French writer André Maurois claims it was a cow; others, a view of the children's ward at St. Mary's. Whatever it was, the painting, submitted under a fictitious name, was thought good enough to exhibit in a London art gallery. The artist was praised by one critic for his "sophisticated naivety." Gray was delighted by the success of the ruse, which was later exposed. As for Fleming, he felt a bit embarrassed by the whole thing and gave a friend some money to buy the picture back for him.

But Fleming's career as an artist was just beginning. He would soon create fascinating paintings using the bright pigments created by germ cultures in his laboratory. These enchanting works, that friends called "Fleming's bacterial rock gardens," were a whimsical wedding of science and art. Throughout his life, Fleming saw no difference between the artist's vision and that of the scientist. Both had to be creative and see the world differently from other people, he believed. "Most scientists are artists in a sense," he later wrote. "Unless they have vision they can do comparatively little with their formulae."

The Chelsea Arts Club, where Fleming was now a member, would become the social mainstay of his life. There he would while away many a happy hour after work, playing cards or snooker, a type of pool, with friends. The artists were fond of their clever medical chum whom they often went to for medical advice. They called him their "Honorary Bacteriologist."

Fleming's first triumph as a bacteriologist, however, was not one that would rank with the achievements of Pasteur and Koch. The future discoverer of penicillin went to work to find a cure for a disease that is not considered particularly serious, except by the millions of teenagers who contract it—acne.

Acne is a disease that inflames oil-producing skin glands, causing the skin to erupt. Fleming succeeded in isolating three different bacteria that cause acne, each causing a different strain of the disease. He experimented with different vaccines made from cultures of the acne microbes, after examining the patient's blood to detect which kind of acne he or she had. Fleming published his results in the medical journal *The Lancet* in April 1909. He concluded that:

> *We may take it as definitely proved that in localized infection, when one inoculates the patient with appropriate doses of a carefully prepared vaccine derived from the infecting organisms, one obtains a beneficial effect.*

This "beneficial effect" was not a complete cure of the disease, but it did clear up the skin temporarily. Through his work with acne, Fleming became something of a skin specialist at a surgery, or medical office, in the West End of London, which he shared with his good friend Pannett. The fact that he was able to attend patients at the surgery while carrying a full load of work at the inoculation department attests to his hardy constitution and his amazing capacity for work.

From acne, Fleming turned his attention to a much more serious disease—syphilis. Syphilis is a deadly venereal disease transmitted by sexual intercourse or from an infected mother to her unborn baby, and it was long thought to be incurable. But in 1909 Paul Ehrlich, a German bacteriologist, discovered Salvarsan, a chemical that could kill the syphilis microbes without injuring the afflicted cells of the body. This was the "magic bullet" that the medical world had long been searching for. By discovering Salvarsan, Ehrlich gave birth to chemotherapy—the treatment of disease by means of microbe-killing chemicals. Today chemotherapy is used successfully in the treatment of cancer and other serious diseases.

Wright and Ehrlich were friends and because of their association, St. Mary's became the first hospital in Britain to receive a supply of Salvarsan. Fleming and Wright's other assistants had the honor of being the first English doctors to treat syphilis patients with Ehrlich's "magic bullet." Most patients asked for Fleming to administer the drug. His deft touch with a needle was becoming well known in the wards. This led his friend Gray to sketch a cartoon of Fleming in his London Scottish Volunteer uniform, complete with kilts and a cigarette dangling from his lips, holding a giant syringe instead of a rifle.

But Fleming was not content to be merely a conduit for someone else's discovery. He found the method used to diagnose syphilis—the "Wassermann reaction"—too complicated and ungainly. He simplified the test and published his results in a *Lancet* article, "A Simple Method of Serum Diagnosis of Syphilis." In it he wrote:

> *The method described is a clinical method, requiring only the preparation of a suitable tissue extract and an elementary knowledge of laboratory method . . . In cases after treatment the reaction may be negative, probably indicating the disappearance of the infection.*

All this work left little time for play. Although he had been a faithful member of the Scottish Volunteers for over a decade, in April 1914, at age 32, Fleming regretfully handed in his resignation. Four months later war broke out in Europe—a war of such magnitude as the world had never seen before. Fleming's old regiment was quickly mobilized and sent to France to fight. Many would never return.

But Fleming too would serve, not on the front line but in a capacity perhaps far more important—as a doctor attending to the wounded and dying. He and his mentor would have the opportunity to put their theories on fighting infection to the test on a scale they could never before have imagined.

CHAPTER 4 NOTES

p. 23   "Of all the evils . . ." Quoted in L. J. Ludovici, *Fleming: Discoverer of Penicillin,* p. 36.

p. 23   "Being a Scot . . ." André Maurois, *The Life of Sir Alexander Fleming,* p. 34.

pp. 25–26   "People don't usually like those . . ." Maurois, *The Life of Sir Alexander Fleming,* p. 72.

p. 29   "We may take it . . ." Maurois, *The Life of Sir Alexander Fleming,* p. 50.

p. 30   "The method described . . ." Ludovici, *Fleming,* p. 59.

5

THE WOUNDS OF WAR

In this war we have found ourselves back among the infections of the Middle Ages.

—Sir Alfred Keogh, head of the Army Medical Services

Almroth Wright wasted no time in offering his services to his country. He was commissioned a colonel in the Army Medical Services and sent to a British army general hospital hastily set up in the seaport of Boulogne in northern France. There he was invited to establish a research laboratory to study the treatment of war wounds. Along with other members of St. Mary's inoculation department, Fleming accompanied Wright and was commissioned a lieutenant. He would prove invaluable to Wright, moving steadily from a trusted aide to a dependable partner in the fight against disease.

France, an ally of England's in World War I, saw fierce fighting against invading German troops. Thousands of young British soldiers were sent to the front in France, and thousands fell dead or wounded on the battlefield. Early optimism about a quick end to the fighting soon faded, and the British dug in for a long, bloody conflict.

This time the army listened to Wright's plea for immunization, and 10 million doses of his antityphoid vaccine were prepared and given to British troops. As a result, typhoid deaths during the war were kept to 1,200—one-tenth of what they would have been without the vaccine.

But Wright saw the war as more than an opportunity to prove the importance of his vaccine. He saw it as a rare chance to study septic wounds and learn how to best treat them. *Septic* is derived from the Greek word *septikos,* meaning "rotted." A septic wound is one that has been poisoned, or made rotten by bacteria that enters it. Many of the wounds suffered on the battlefield were minor when compared to the dreadful infections that could fester in them by the time the patients arrived at the hospital in Boulogne.

The field hospital was set up in the Casino, a once-elegant building that had seen better days. Wright's unit was relegated to two bathrooms in the basement. There their lab regularly flooded with stinking water from a drainpipe. Working conditions quickly became intolerable. Wright exerted his considerable influence and soon the little lab was quickly moved to the top floor of the Casino, which had once been a fencing school. Fleming went to work improvising the lab, putting together instruments and equipment out of whatever was at hand. He devised alcohol-fueled Bunsen burners and paraffin-heated incubators. Makeshift and modest as it was, years later Fleming called it one of the best laboratories he had ever worked in.

At the time, standard treatment for septic wounds was literally to drown them in antiseptics—the powerful germ-killing chemicals introduced by Lister. These agents were thought to kill all germs they came in contact with and to prevent the spread of infection. Wright and Fleming, who still believed that the body's natural immune system was superior to any chemical, began a thorough study of wounds of the soldiers brought into the hospital. What they found out was truly startling.

Carbolic acid, iodine, and other antiseptics, they discovered, while useful in superficial cuts, did not kill infections in more serious wounds. In fact, antiseptics actually made the infections worse. Patients whose wounds were not treated with antiseptics stood a better chance of recovering than those who were.

How could this be? Fleming believed that the antiseptics were destroying the white blood cells, or phagocytes, instead of the invading microbes. These antiseptics were wiping out the body's only defense against the germs. To prove his theory, Fleming took two test tubes and filled one with microbes and carbolic acid and the other with blood and microbes. When he

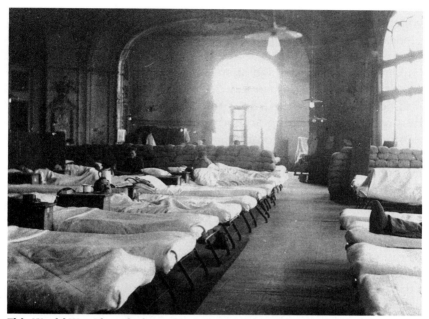

This World War I hospital ward in France captures the stark conditions that Fleming worked under at the Boulogne hospital. Note the wall of sandbags to prevent flying glass from injuring the patients in case of an enemy attack. (Yale University Medical Library)

added carbolic acid to the second mixture, the germs gradually increased in number. The antiseptic was strengthening the infection by killing off the defending phagocytes in the blood.

But Fleming discovered another reason for the antiseptic's failure to stop infection—the very nature of the wounds themselves. A "clean," superficial wound was a rarity in the Boulogne hospital. The exploding shells and flying shrapnel of the battlefield caused deep, jagged wounds that medical doctors had never seen before. André Maurois describes the war wounds that Fleming and Wright saw as having "corners and crannies which might be compared to the configuration of the Norwegian fjords." Such wounds were the perfect breeding ground for infection, offering deadly germs a thousand hiding places from applied antiseptics.

Further complicating matters, shrapnel entering the body picked up bits of germ-ridden clothing, mud, and vegetable matter that were often embedded deep inside the wound. Fleming compared pieces of clothing taken from wounds with germs found in the wounds. He discovered that the clothing itself contained germs of lockjaw and gangrene; when soldiers were wounded, the germs were transferred to the wound.

"Because the projectile has produced a very extensive destruction of tissue," Fleming argued in a *Lancet* article published in September 1915, war wounds were far worse than ordinary ones. "Not only do dead tissues provide a good culture medium for microbes, they actually prevent the healthy phagocytes from reaching them," he wrote.

Fleming and Wright's solution to the problem was to prohibit wounds from being treated with antiseptics. They advocated the surgical removal of all dead tissue and other foreign matter from the wound, followed by a thorough washing with a sterile salt solution. This would not only clean out the wound but promote the flow of white blood cells. Then they recommended the application of a sterile dressing to keep out any further infection.

This sound, scientific thinking was based on long hours of observation and experiment. It was argued convincingly by Fleming in several published papers and by Wright in addresses to the Royal Society of Medicine and other learned bodies. The medical community politely read and listened and then went right back to using antiseptics. They stubbornly clung to the belief that antiseptics were the best defense against infection. If one antiseptic failed to halt the infection, they reasoned, it was because it wasn't strong enough and a more powerful one was needed. The fight between nature and chemicals was in full swing once more. Wright was so detested by many of his peers for daring to question established practice that they attempted to have him recalled from France and stripped of his commission. Fortunately they failed.

As for Fleming, he found respite from the war on a visit home. He returned to the London house he had continued to share with his brothers and sisters in the prewar years. The Flemings introduced him to a new friend and neighbor—a handsome, blue-eyed, blond Irishwoman named Sarah McElroy. Together with her twin sister Elizabeth, Sarah—whom everyone affectionately called Sally—ran a private nursing home on Baker Street, not far from where the Flemings lived. Sally was a lively, talkative extrovert, the direct opposite of the quiet, introverted Alec. As often happens, these two very different people were immediately attracted to each other. Sally brought Alec out of himself and he loved her for it. She, on her part, respected the strength of his character and saw fine things in his future. "Alec is a great man," she told friends, "but nobody knows it."

They were married two days before Christmas in 1915. The new couple settled in an apartment, or flat, in London. Then Alec returned to Boulogne and Sally went back to running her nursing home. Elizabeth McElroy moved into the Fleming home to care for the ill Grace Fleming, who had moved in with her children some years earlier. John Fleming, one of Alec's older brothers, fell in love with his mother's nurse and Alec's sister-in-law. Again, it was a case of opposites attracting. John was outgoing and Elizabeth, quiet and somber.

Back in France, Fleming's colleagues would not believe that the dour Scotsman had actually married. Even after he showed them a photograph of Sally, they were skeptical.

On his return to France, Fleming found his commanding officer as eccentric as ever. The great Sir Almroth rarely bothered wearing a uniform, was careless about his dress, and once was gently admonished by his orderly sergeant for going around with a hole in the seat of his pants. His behavior also hardly became a military man. On one memorable occasion a group of visiting French army doctors were aghast when they entered a room to find the 55-year-old Wright wrestling on the floor with Fleming!

A more acceptable form of recreation as the war began to wind down was golf. No one enjoyed the game more than Fleming. But, as with other games, he was never content to play it by the rules. He was forever making up his own rules, challenging himself in new and unexpected ways. Recalls his old friend Pannett: "he delighted in making difficulties for himself, just for the fun of overcoming them. For instance, he once undertook to play a round of golf using only one club," rather than the usual 14 clubs golfers nowadays choose from, depending on the type of shot needed.

There were other diversions amid the carnage of war. Wright's friends came to visit and discuss his latest research, just as they had at St. Mary's. Among those who came to call in Boulogne were the ever-faithful Shaw and the American brain specialist Henry Cushing.

The war finally ended on November 11, 1918—Armistice Day. It was a time for celebration but also sober reflection. In four years of fighting, 8 million soldiers had died on the battlefield and in field hospitals. Wright and Fleming had reason to be both proud and saddened by their ground-breaking work on war wounds. Although their suggested treatment of wounds had been ignored, it would become accepted and save tens of thousands of lives in the next world war, which would shake Europe 21 years later.

But the dying in this war was not over. Just months before the armistice, a deadly strain of influenza appeared in Spain and quickly spread across Europe and to the United States. In October a second wave of influenza struck, far deadlier than the first. By the end of 1918 over 20 million people were dead from the dreaded disease—over twice the number killed in the war. The epidemic drove home a grim truth for Fleming and the rest of the medical team at Boulogne. War between nations could be ended with a peace treaty, but there could no be armistice in the war against disease. It was an ongoing struggle that could be won only by one small victory at a time, achieved through painstaking research and experiment.

Those dead from influenza now far outnumbered the wounded, and in his last days in Boulogne Fleming had to carry the dead to the cemetery himself. "Surrounded by all those infected wounds, by men who were suffering and dying without our being able to do anything to help them," he later wrote, "I was consumed by a desire to discover, after all this struggling and waiting, something which would kill those microbes, something like Salvarsan . . ."

That "something" would be penicillin. But it would be another 10 years before Fleming would discover it. In the meantime, another discovery lay ahead of him. In its own way, it would prove to be as remarkable a medical find as penicillin itself.

CHAPTER 5 NOTES

p. 31   "In this war we have found . . ." André Maurois, *The Life of Sir Alexander Fleming,* p. 85.

p. 34   "Because the projectile has produced . . ." Maurois, *The Life of Sir Alexander Fleming,* p. 86.

p. 35   "he delighted in making difficulties . . ." Maurois, *The Life of Sir Alexander Fleming,* p. 32.

p. 36   "Surrounded by all those infected wounds . . ." Maurois, *The Life of Sir Alexander Fleming,* p. 101.

6

THE BODY'S SECRET WEAPON—LYSOZYME

Early on, Fleming began to tease me about my excessive tidiness in the laboratory . . . I took his teasing in the spirit in which it was given. However, the sequel was to prove how right he was, for if he had been as tidy as he thought I was, he would never have made his two great discoveries—lysozyme and penicillin.

—V. D. Allison in a 1974 lecture

In January 1919 Alexander Fleming returned to St. Mary's Hospital a very different man from the one who had left four and a half years earlier. He was no longer one of Almroth Wright's bright young men but a respected bacteriologist in his own right. He had published a dozen noteworthy papers on war wounds, the result of significant and ground-breaking research. Indeed, medical experts today believe his war work with antiseptics ranks among his greatest achievements.

To demonstrate his new status as a scientist, Fleming was invited in February 1919 to give the Royal College of Surgeons' honored Hunterian Lecture. His speech was entitled "The Action of Physical and Physiological Antiseptics in a Septic Wound." It was a brilliant, concise summary of his work at Boulogne and made a convincing argument against the use of antiseptics in infected wounds. If his august audience wasn't convinced, this was probably due as much to his weak delivery as to the content of his speech. Unlike his mentor, Fleming was not a forceful speaker.

The idea of drawing undue attention to himself went against the grain of his modest nature. While modesty might be an admirable trait in most people, it is deadly in a speaker who has important information to communicate. Fleming himself was keenly aware of this flaw.

"It's a pity I have not the gift of tongues, it's worth more than anything else just to be able to talk," he once mused. "You know, with some men the words just flow out, and would charm a bird off a bush. But I was brought up wrongly for that."

Yet his achievements were undeniable, and they brought him new honors at St. Mary's. He was appointed assistant lecturer in bacteriology, and two years later Wright himself named Fleming assistant director of the inoculation department. This promotion came as a bitter blow to his old friend and fellow marksman John Freeman. Freeman felt that Wright had promised him the assistant-ship and for a time blamed Fleming for maneuvering to steal it from him. Nothing, of course, could be further from the truth. If anyone was to blame, it was Wright himself, who had a nasty habit of pitting his subordinates against one another. Fleming used his new power wisely. He avoided quarrels and managed to support Wright, while keeping a sympathetic ear turned to his colleagues and their complaints. At times, it was a difficult balancing act.

With his new position and the added income from Sally's sale of her nursing home, the Flemings were ready to buy a second home in the country. There they could relax on weekends and summers from the cares and pressures of the city. On a visit with friends in Suffolk, they stopped at an auction at a country home in the village of Barton Mills. They went to buy a few antiques and ended up buying the house instead. They called it, for some unexplained reason, the Dhoon, and it remained Fleming's refuge from city life for the next 34 years. The quaint Georgian-style cottage came with a three-acre garden, a small river for fishing, and a tennis court. Both Sally and Alec had green thumbs and soon went to work turning the overgrown garden into a veritable Eden of flowers and vegetables.

"A gardener must never be impatient," Fleming was fond of saying,

Flowers grow in their own time and one does more harm than good if he tries to hasten the process. One can protect them against the weather: one can see that they get food and drink, but it is only too easy to kill them when either is too strong or too plentiful. They are responsive to kindness, but they can also withstand any amount of hard treatment. In other words, they are like human beings.

Alec was as busy experimenting on his plants as he was on the microbes in his laboratory. He astonished visitors with his uncanny ability to make things grow under the most unlikely conditions. He would casually cut a shoot from a tree and stick it in the ground, and it would take root at once.

The couple loved to entertain, and nearly every weekend in the summer the house was humming with guests. Alec enjoyed arranging games and field trips. One of his more spectacular innovations was midnight croquet played by the light of candlelit hoops. But it was Sally who was the real dynamo at the Dhoon, which her husband readily admitted. "She does all the work," he once said, "and provides all the conversation."

In the autumn of 1921, the usually healthy Fleming caught a bad cold. That in itself was nothing unusual, but it led to a most unusual discovery.

Fleming, like the other bacteriologists in Wright's lab, was his own best guinea pig. In the prewar days, they would often try out new vaccines on themselves, sometimes with serious consequences. At least two doctors in the department died from infections contracted from experimental vaccines. "We were the human pin-cushions, we stuck things in ourselves so often," recalled Dr. Leonard Colebrook, one of Fleming's colleagues.

In this case, Fleming saw his cold as an opportunity to study the microbe that caused it. Each day he took some of his own nasal mucus, put it on a glass plate, and examined it carefully under the microscope. He went into the lab one day a few weeks later and looked at some Petri dishes that contained the mucus. One dish had large yellow colonies of microbes growing in it. This in itself was not extraordinary. Fleming was notorious for not cleaning up his dishes, and all sorts of germs found a home in them. But, for some reason, there were no microbes to be found at all near the nasal mucus.

Dr. V. D. Allison, a young Irish assistant, was standing nearby. "This is interesting," Fleming said to him, showing him the dish. Something in his nasal secretions killed the microbes around it, Fleming believed. Many years later, Allison explained what happened next:

> Fleming's next step was to test the effect of fresh nasal mucus on the germ, but this time he prepared an opaque, yellow suspension of the germ in saline and added some nasal mucus to it. To our surprise the opaque suspension became in the space of less than two minutes as clear as water . . . it was an astonishing and thrilling moment [and] the beginning of an investigation which occupied us for the next few years.

Fleming knew he was onto something big, something that might turn out to be as important in the fight against microbes as the opsonic index or Salvarsan. Here was a natural antiseptic produced by the human body that appeared to be more powerful than carbolic acid or any other chemical antiseptic.

If mucus contained this germicidal agent, what about other bodily secretions? Fleming took some of his own tears and tested them. A single teardrop dissolved a colony of microbes in under five seconds. "I had never seen anything like it," wrote the astonished scientist.

Allison recalled the next five weeks vividly:

> . . . my tears and his were our main supply of material for experimenting. Many were the lemons we had to buy to produce all those tears! We used to cut a small piece of lemon-peel and squeeze it into our eyes, looking into the mirror of the microscope.

But more tears were required for the work than two grown men could provide. Puzzled visitors and eager lab boys were enlisted in what Fleming humorously referred to as the "ordeal by lemon." The lab boys were paid three pence for each good cry. "If you cry often enough, you'll soon be able to retire!" Fleming told one red-eyed contributor.

In December Fleming wrote a paper on his work with this amazing substance and delivered it before the Medical Research Club. The response was the same as that which followed his talk at the College of Surgeons two years earlier. Gwyn Macfarlane, in his excellent biography of Fleming, has written: "What would later be regarded as an historic event in medical history seemed to have sunk without a ripple."

But Fleming had too much faith in himself to be discouraged. This was *his* discovery, not Wright's or anyone else, and he would not abandon it. He tried the same experiment using human saliva and got the same amazing results. Next he turned to human tissue—a scrap of skin, a few hairs, even a nail paring. All of them killed germs with efficient speed. In his lectures at the medical school, Fleming would hand each student a test tube containing colonies of germs. Then he would tell them to cut off a piece of fingernail and place it into the bacterial-clouded test tube. By the end of the lecture, the paring had killed all the bacteria and the liquid had become completely clear.

If human bodies contained such protection, why not animals too? Fleming reasoned. He found the same substance at work in dog saliva, horse and cow tears, and the sperm of several animals. If animals, not why plants? Fleming expanded his experiments to include flowers and vegetables from his Suffolk garden. They tested positive. The vegetable with the highest concentration of the germ-killing substance, interestingly enough, was a turnip.

But he discovered the richest concentration of the germicide in the white part of birds' eggs. The substance was 100 times more concentrated in egg white than in tears and was capable of killing the strongest of bacteria. Even when diluted 60 million times in water, the egg white still retained enough of the germ killer to destroy some germs. Birds' eggs were not the only eggs that contained this powerful germicide. While fishing one weekend at the Dhoon, Fleming caught a pike and found its eggs also contained the agent. So did many other fish eggs.

This research led Fleming to a startling conclusion. "I realized that every living thing must, *in all its parts,* have an effective defense-mechanism," he wrote; "otherwise, no living organism could continue to exist. The bacteria would invade and destroy it."

By February 1922, Fleming felt he was ready to present his findings to the "Old Man." Wright had slowed down since the war and was no longer the dynamo in the laboratory he had once been, but he immediately saw the value of Fleming's discovery. He agreed to submit Fleming's paper on his work to the Royal Society, the world's oldest and most prestigious body of scientists. But the substance needed a name. Wright, as always, rose to the occasion. He dubbed it lysozyme—*lyso,* from the Greek *lysis,* meaning "to dissolve" (which is what it did to microbes), and *zyme,* because its actions clearly related it to the enzymes—chemical substances in living cells that cause change in other substances without being changed themselves.

The paper, "On a Remarkable Bacteriolytic Element Found in Tissues and Secretions," was delivered by Wright himself at a meeting of the Royal Society. The response was little better than Fleming had received. Even Wright's dramatic delivery couldn't stir the imagination of the nation's leading scientists. This wasn't really his fault, nor Fleming's. Whether lysozyme worked or not mattered little to most medical men. As yet, they could see no practical use for it.

Later that year, Wright nominated his younger colleague for election to the Fellowship of the Royal Society, of which he himself was a member. The society was impressed by Fleming's work but didn't see it as being important enough to elect him to their membership. His name was put on a long waiting list, where it remained for the next 20 years.

But Fleming would not be discouraged. With Allison's assistance, he continued experimenting with lysozyme. He injected a rabbit with lysozyme-rich egg white. It killed germs in the animal's blood for several hours. He even injected egg white into a few patients at St. Mary's with favorable results.

However, Fleming observed that most lysozyme attacked only the weaker bacteria in the body. Why was this? He theorized that thousands of years ago, lysozyme was capable of killing all bacteria, but over time, a few germs built up resistance to it. Eventually, these resistant germs became the deadly microbes that we know and fear today. It was a fascinating theory, but one that was, of course, unprovable.

Fleming faced another problem—getting enough lysozyme to make it practical in fighting disease. To solve this dilemma he had to find a way to extract the substance from egg whites and other substances. But this was a job for a chemist, not a bacteriologist. Unfortunately, St. Mary's had no chemist or biochemist on its staff.

Then in 1926, a young doctor named Frederick Ridley came to the hospital. Ridley wasn't a chemist, but he had studied chemistry and knew more about it than any other doctor at St. Mary's. Fleming asked him to help, and Ridley obliged by trying to extract lysozyme. He failed.

"It is a pity," Fleming said, "because if we had this substance pure, it ought to be possible to maintain in the body a concentration which would kill certain bacteria."

Fleming never gave up on lysozyme. He published eight papers on the substance, the last in 1932. Five years later an organic chemist at Oxford University, E. A. H. Roberts, finally succeeded in extracting semipure lysozyme.

Since then, lysozyme has been the subject of much interest and study. Over 2,000 scientific papers to date have been written about it. It is used today to protect certain foods, such as Russian caviar, from contamination. Doctors also use it in the treatment of eye and intestinal diseases.

For all its value, lysozyme would not be the panacea—or cure-all—that Fleming had hoped for. Yet it encouraged him to keep on looking for the magical substance that would kill the deadliest of microbes without harming the body's tissue. And one autumn day in 1928, he found it.

CHAPTER 6 NOTES

p. 39   "Early on, Fleming began to tease me . . ." Gwyn Macfarlane, *Alexander Fleming: The Man and the Myth*, p. 99.

p. 40   "A gardener must never be impatient . . ." André Maurois, *The Life of Sir Alexander Fleming*, p. 101.

p. 42   "Fleming's next step was to test . . ." Macfarlane, *Alexander Fleming,* pp. 99–100.

p. 42   "I had never seen . . ." Maurois, *The Life of Sir Alexander Fleming,* p. 111.

p. 42   "my tears and his were our main supply . . ." Maurois, *The Life of Sir Alexander Fleming,* p. 110.

p. 43   "What would later be regarded . . ." Macfarlane, *Alexander Fleming,* p. 103.

p. 43   "I realized that every living thing . . ." Maurois, *The Life of Sir Alexander Fleming,* p. 114.

p. 45   "It is a pity . . ." Maurois, *The Life of Sir Alexander Fleming,* p. 119.

7
UNFINISHED BUSINESS

One day someone will find a way of isolating the active principle, and of producing it on a large scale. Then we shall see it regularly used against the diseases caused by organisms which, I know, it can destroy.

> —Fleming in a conversation in 1937 with a friend, Dr. Laidlaw, about the potential of penicillin

His discovery of penicillin in the autumn of 1928 gave Alexander Fleming a new purpose and direction. Here was another natural substance, like lysozyme, that could strengthen the body's defenses against bacteria and other microorganisms and kill them while leaving the cells of the body unharmed. Penicillin was the first antibiotic—a drug produced by microbes that can be used to fight disease-causing microbes. People had used molds and the antibiotic agents they formed to fight skin infections for at least 2,500 years. But before Fleming's discovery, no one really understood what antibiotics were.

Fleming was determined this time that his discovery would become more than a mere medical curiosity, and he dropped all other work to concentrate on penicillin. He set up a special lab exclusively for experiments with the drug and enlisted two young assistants to help him.

His experiments led him to make new discoveries about penicillin. He found that 20 degrees Centigrade was the ideal temperature to grow penicillin in and that as the temperature went up, the drug's strength as a germ killer steadily diminished. He also found out that adding tiny amounts of acid to the broth stimulated penicillin's growth.

On January 9, 1929, Fleming noted in his laboratory notebook the success of his first experiment with penicillin on a human subject. Stuart Craddock, his colleague, was suffering from an infected sinus. When Fleming applied the penicillin broth to the infected area, it cleared up immediately. Craddock was by now as enthusiastic about the magical properties of penicillin as Fleming himself. He called it "the antiseptic of his [Fleming's] dreams."

A second experiment on the open leg wound of a woman who had been in a car accident, however, failed to halt the infection. "The practical difficulty in the use of penicillin for dressings of septic wounds," Fleming wrote a few years later, "is the amount of trouble necessary for its preparation and the difficulty of maintaining its potency for more than a few weeks." To be more effective and stable, penicillin had to be purified and concentrated.

All Fleming's skill as a bacteriologist couldn't help him to remove the impurities from the drug. To isolate penicillin he needed the expertise of a chemist. Frederick Ridley, who had tried to help isolate lysozyme, again volunteered to work on penicillin. Ridley's plan was to evaporate the liquid in the mold juice, leaving the solid penicillin behind. But if he heated the mixture, the penicillin would be destroyed. So, with Craddock's help, he evaporated the broth by means of a cold vacuum. When the process was completed, there was a thick, brown mass at the bottom of the experimental flask. When tested, this syrup, which they humorously called "melted toffee," proved to be up to fifty times stronger than the broth.

Craddock later recalled what followed:

> We were full of hope when we started, but, as we went on, week after week after week, we could get nothing but this glutinous mass which, quite apart from anything else, would not keep. The concentrated product retained its power for about a week, but after a fortnight [two weeks] it became inert . . . We could not know at the time that we had only one more hurdle to cross. We had been so often discouraged. We thought we had got the Thing. We put it in the refrigerator, only to find, after a week, that it had begun to vanish. Had an experienced chemist come on the scene, I think we would have got across that last hurdle. Then we could have published our result. But the expert did not materialize.

Craddock soon left for a better position at another laboratory. Ridley took a long cruise for health reasons. But Fleming doggedly continued to work on penicillin.

On February 13, 1929, he went public with his discovery and presented a paper on penicillin to the Medical Research Club. He made a convincing argument for penicillin as an effective antiseptic against disease. He ended his talk by telling the roomful of medical experts that "I may be wrong, but I believe that penicillin although produced by a humble mold, will turn out to be a safe and most effective germ killer."

As before with his lectures on lysozyme, Fleming's delivery was weak and apologetic. According to Sir Henry Dale, the club's chairman, "He was very shy and excessively modest in his presentation, he gave it in a half-hearted sort of way, shrugging his shoulders as though he were deprecating the importance of what he said . . ." However, Dale continued, "the elegance and beauty of his observations made a great impression." If this was so, the impression did nothing to stimulate interest in penicillin. When Fleming had finished talking, not a comment was made, not a question was asked by the distinguished audience. It was, in Fleming's words a "frightful moment," but one that didn't shake his faith in penicillin or himself.

Several months later, he prepared a report on penicillin for the *British Journal of Experimental Pathology*. In the report, he emphasized penicillin's antibacterial power and its nontoxic effect on the body's cells and tissues, and he advocated its use as an antiseptic. By talking and writing about his discovery, Fleming hoped to draw the attention of others in the medical field to experiment and test penicillin. The plan worked.

Professor Harold Raistrick, one of the country's finest chemists, became interested in Fleming's discovery. He was less interested, however, in penicillin itself than in the fact that it was derived from a mold. Raistrick, who taught biochemistry at the London School of Hygiene and Tropical Medicine, was a leading expert in the study of mold chemistry. In early 1930 he approached Fleming for a sample of his original *Penicillium* mold, which the bacteriologist eagerly offered. Like Craddock and Ridley, Raistrick tried to evaporate the liquid part of the broth, but he first dissolved it in ether, a colorless liquid that could easily evaporate and is often used as a solvent. Then he evaporated the ether with air. What remained was a solid yellow substance that, much to Raistrick's chagrin, had no germ-killing properties at all. The penicillin had vanished into thin air. "It was unbelievable," Raistrick later wrote. "We could do nothing in the face of it, so we dropped it and went on with our other investigations and experiments."

There were other, more personal reasons, that ended the experiments. One of Raistrick's assistants, a biochemist, died suddenly. Another, R. Lovell, a bacteriologist, left Raistrick's department to enroll in veterinary school.

Lovell later had this to say about his work on penicillin:

> *I think that our main contribution had been to show that the mould could be cultivated in a synthetic medium; that it was possible to keep it longer when the pH* had been brought over on to the acid side, and that we could remove the penicillin by extraction with ether. It was a great misfortune that Clutterbuck [the other assistant] died while still a young man. I feel quite sure that, had he lived, it would not have been long before he would have realized that by switching the pH over to the alkaline side he would have been able to recover the penicillin which was apparently lost when we treated the filtrate with ether . . .*

But Raistrick's experiments had brought out two other valuable facts about penicillin. One, he had discovered that the penicillin-producing mold was not *Penicillium rubrum*, as Fleming's colleague LaTouche had claimed, but a rarer variety, *Penicillium notatum*. Second, and more important, Raistrick discovered that the golden substance that contained penicillin, was of itself completely ineffective in killing germs. The "yellow magic" that some Fleming supporters spoke of was a misnomer.

Fleming was disappointed by Raistrick's failure, but not deterred. He used penicillin as a local agent in ointment or liquid form on any patient at St. Mary's whom he thought could benefit from it. He also gave some of the mold juice to another staff doctor, who used it successfully to treat babies with eye infections and a coal miner with an eye injury. But these were small victories that barely

---

* A number indicating the level of acidity in a substance.

tapped the vast potential of penicillin. Years later Fleming admitted, "We tried it tentatively on a few old sinuses in hospital, and though the reports were favorable there was nothing miraculous."

He was well aware that to become an effective drug, penicillin had to be concentrated in a form that could be mass-produced, preserved, and stored for use in hospitals everywhere. Until this could be done, the substance would remain a medical curiosity like lysozyme. A miracle was what Fleming needed to isolate his elusive drug and release its enormous potential. But months and years passed, and the miracle didn't happen.

By 1932, Fleming could write with some confidence in the *Journal of Pathology* that in the treatment of septic wounds penicillin "certainly appeared to be superior to dressings containing potent chemicals." But he was already turning his attention away from penicillin to other matters. When elected president of the Section of Pathology in the Royal Society of Medicine,* the subject of Fleming's presidential address was not penicillin but lysozyme.

Yet there were other matters to take Fleming's mind off this great disappointment. There was the regular, if less satisfying, routine work in the laboratory and pleasant weekends at the Dhoon with his family. The Flemings now had a child—a son, Robert, born in 1924. He would be their only child. Fleming adored his son and even gave up his beloved game of golf to spend more time with him. Still, there were times when other activities overtook the responsibilities of parenthood. A friend, Dr. Gerald Willcox, remembered one such time:

> One day, at the Dhoon, he took me out fishing in a boat with his small son. All of a sudden he hooked a pike. The boy, mad with excitement, jumped up, and fell into the river. Fleming remained seated, his attention divided between the pike, which was fighting like a mad thing, and me, for I was trying to fish the child out of the water; but not for a moment did he let go of his rod . . .

Sally could be just as stubborn. One day, not liking her nephews and nieces calling her "Aunt Sally," she decided to change her

---

* This organization is not to be confused with the world-famous Royal Society that still denied Fleming membership.

name to "Sareen." And Sareen she stayed to everyone who knew her for the rest of her life.

In the early 1930s, St. Mary's Medical School underwent a long-overdue major renovation, thanks to the generosity of the English press magnate Lord Beaverbrook. (Years later Beaverbrook would become Fleming's personal champion and help make his name a household word through his newspapers.) As part of the renovation program, the inoculation department got a new building and a spacious laboratory, carefully planned out by Wright and Fleming.

King George V and Queen Mary attended the official opening in 1933. The staff enthusiastically decorated the building for the memorable occasion. Fleming contributed a generous display of his famous "germ paintings." The queen, on seeing these eccentric artworks, lost her regal bearing and declared, "Yes—but what *good* is it?" Such a thought would have never occurred to the artist, who saw artistic beauty, unlike scientific research, as an end in itself.

The following year, Lewis Holt, a biochemist, joined Wright's staff. Fleming's hopes for isolating penicillin were raised once more. The biochemist agreed to have a try at purifying penicillin. He actually got farther than Raistrick in isolating the elusive substance, but in the end penicillin's lack of stability proved too frustrating for him. Fleming was not deeply disappointed this time. It was what he had come to expect. His hopes for his "wonder drug" had been slowly fading over the past few years, although he never gave up completely.

In any event, other matters were occupying his time and energies. He was busy writing one section of an ambitious new book, *Recent Advances in Serum and Vaccine Therapy*. In 1935 he took a trip to Iraq to attend the ceremonial opening of a new oil pipeline and stopped on the way in Rome to attend a medical congress. And then that same year came a medical discovery that seemed to put penicillin in the shadows forever.

A German doctor and chemist, Gerhard Domagk, announced his discovery of a red dye that killed certain germs in humans and animals with amazing efficiency. He called his discovery Prontosil. It was the first long-anticipated chemical "magic bullet" since

Fleming examines one of his culture dishes of penicillin. Although he discovered the antibiotic in 1928, it would be 12 long years before penicillin was successfully purified for practical use. (UPI/Bettmann)

Ehrlich had discovered Salvarsan years earlier. Prontosil was to be only the first of a number of synthetic chemicals called sulfonamides that would herald a new age of medical treatment that began with Salvarsan—chemotherapy. To the dismay of Fleming, Wright, and their supporters, artificial chemicals—not natural substances and the body's own immune system—were suddenly winning the war against disease.

Fleming might have been justifiably bitter, but it is a measure of the man that he was not. He saw the sulfonamides as a tool in the fight against disease that could not be ignored. He even experimented with the chemicals himself, putting them through some of the same tests he tried on penicillin. The results were mixed. On one hand, the chemicals were amazingly efficient at killing certain kinds of bacteria. On the other hand, many bacteria were not affected by them, and among those that were, there was reason to believe some strains would build up a resistance with time. Prontosil also caused some negative side effects that still plague chemotherapy today, such as nausea and vomiting.

All in all, Fleming still believed that penicillin would one day be a far more effective germ killer than any chemical. But when would that day come? The sulfonamides could be purified easily and had proved their practicality. Penicillin had not.

In that same crucial year of 1935, two men arrived at Oxford University who would pick up where Fleming left off. One was an Australian pathologist, the other, a Jewish chemist fleeing the Nazis in Germany. Together, they would make Fleming's dream a reality.

CHAPTER 7 NOTES

p. 47   "One day someone will find a way . . ." André Maurois, *The Life of Sir Alexander Fleming,* p. 154.

p. 48   "We were full of hope . . ." Maurois, *The Life of Sir Alexander Fleming*, p. 135–136.

p. 49   "He was very shy . . ." Maurois, *The Life of Sir Alexander Fleming*, p. 136.

p. 50   "It was unbelievable . . ." Gwyn Macfarlane, *Alexander Fleming: The Man and the Myth*, p. 143.

p. 50   "I think that our main contribution . . ." Maurois, *The Life of Sir Alexander Fleming*, p. 139.

p. 51   "We tried it tentatively . . ." L. J. Ludovici, *Fleming: Discoverer of Penicillin*, p. 141.

p. 51   "One day, at the Dhoon . . ." Maurois, *The Life of Sir Alexander Fleming*, p. 102.

8

MIRACLE AT OXFORD

You have made something of my substance.

—Alexander Fleming to Ernst Chain after viewing the process whereby Chain isolated penicillin

Fifty miles northwest of London lies Great Britain's oldest and most distinguished institute of higher learning, Oxford University. Its various colleges have attracted great scholars and scientists for centuries. Howard Florey was one of these individuals. Born in Australia in 1898, Florey first went to Oxford on a Rhodes scholarship in 1921. He studied medicine at the university's Magdelen College for three years and then studied pathology at Oxford's principal rival, Cambridge University. The following year he traveled to the United States on a grant as a Rockefeller Traveling Fellow, where he worked as a pathologist in numerous laboratories. Florey soon returned to Cambridge to lecture, and in 1931 moved to the University of Sheffield, where he was named professor of pathology.

It was during this time that Florey first became interested in the work of Alexander Fleming. He read about Fleming's first major discovery—lysozyme—and conducted his own experiments on the substance. In 1935, Florey was appointed professor of pathology at Oxford's Sir William Dunn School. There, under his supervision, E. A. H. Roberts first extracted semipure lysozyme, as mentioned earlier. The same year, Florey invited a gifted 29-year-old chemist, Ernst B. Chain, to run his biochemical department.

Howard Florey, an Australian pathologist who went to Oxford in 1935, led the team that succeeded in isolating penicillin in 1940. (UPI/Bettmann)

Chain was a German Jew, born and raised in Berlin, where his father was a chemical industrialist. Young Chain had studied biochemistry at the University of Berlin. When the Nazis came to power in 1933, a growing wave of anti-Semitism drove Chain and many other Jews to leave Germany. He immigrated to England, where he taught at Cambridge before joining Florey's team at Oxford.

Chain, like Florey, had a strong interest in antibacterial substances and started experimenting with lysozyme. A tireless and meticulous researcher, Chain read through every scientific paper written about germ-killing substances with a microbiological origin. During his research, he came across the 1929 paper on penicillin Fleming had delivered to the Medical Research Club and that was later published in the *British Journal of Experimental Pathology*. Chain described the part fate played in this discovery:

> It was sheer luck that I came across Fleming's paper . . . No chemist would normally think of reading a work on pathology to assist his researches in chemistry, but here in Oxford at the School of Pathology the two subjects are combined under one roof, so they are closely linked and this direct association led me to go through the journal . . .
>
> I made up my mind to see what I could find out about penicillin . . . By a lucky turn of chance I discovered that we had here on the spot, growing in the school, some cultures of the very mold, Penicillium notatum, *which Fleming had grown at St. Mary's Hospital . . .*
>
> So I obtained my culture of the mold and started to work on the problem where Professor Raistrick had left off.

But the experiments Chain planned would take money. He talked to Florey about it, and his boss shared his enthusiasm for the project. Florey applied for a grant from the Rockefeller Foundation, and in a few months they received $5,000 to carry out their experiments.

While Florey and Chain were about to begin their work on penicillin, Fleming was wondering if his discovery would ever amount to anything. Where once friends and colleagues were eager to experiment with the drug, now chemists, such as the professor of pharmacology at St. Mary's, politely declined his requests to try to purify penicillin. Even his mentor and champion, Almroth Wright, offered him no support. Although penicillin was a natural substance, it was not a vaccine. Immunology was still Wright's main interest, and he could no more accept penicillin than he could accept the chemical sulfonamides.

This lack of interest in penicillin extended across the Atlantic. A young American doctor at the Pennsylvania College of Agriculture, like Chain, happened upon Fleming's old paper on penicillin and asked the school for a modest $100 to carry out experiments on the drug for a thesis. Not only was his request denied, but when a sympathetic professor offered to give the young man the money, the school threatened to dismiss him.

It is not surprising that when an American colleague asked Fleming what had become of penicillin, its discoverer had nothing much to say. Alec and Sareen had made their first visit to the United States in August 1939 to attend the Third International Congress of Microbiology in New York City. He delivered a paper at the conference on what had become a pressing issue for him—combating disease by combining vaccines with chemotherapy.

The Flemings intended to spend some time traveling across the United States, but their trip was cut short by shocking news from Europe. On September 3, Britain declared war on Germany in response to the German invasion of Poland. The Flemings returned home on the next boat. As he had 25 years before, Fleming volunteered his services to his government in this time of national crisis.

As a leading bacteriologist with invaluable experie..ce in treating war wounds, Fleming's offer was gratefully accepted. The Ministry of Health employed him to supervise the medical efforts in a large urban district that included London. This time Fleming feared he wouldn't have to travel as far as France to help wounded soldiers. The Germans had the air power and bombing capability to bring the war onto English soil. The casualties would undoubtedly include many civilians. Fleming traveled across the district helping to form hospital teams to prepare for the onslaught. More than once it must have crossed his mind how much better prepared he would be to treat the wounded if he had only been able to purify penicillin.

Meanwhile, unknown to Fleming, Florey, Chain, and their Oxford medical team were working feverishly to do just that. In his work, Florey had discovered that penicillin was an unstable enzyme whose instability was heightened when concentrated by evaporation. Chain therefore decided to try to isolate the substance in a different way from previous chemists. He attempted a new freeze-drying process called lyophilization. The process allowed liquid to pass directly from a solid to a gaseous state in a vacuum. The result of Chain's experiment was a

brown-yellowish powder. While purer than the penicillin derived from previous attempts, it still contained several protein
and salt impurities.

Next Chain tried dissolving the powder in a solution of meth-
anol. While this eliminated some of the remaining impurities,
it also made the penicillin unstable again. Despite this failure,
Florey and Chain felt the penicillin was pure enough to be tested
on animals for toxicity. Florey injected 30 milligrams of the
solution into a mouse. The mouse showed no ill effects. He
repeated the experiment on 20 mice. Not one showed any visible
negative reaction. The men had good reason to take heart.
Although still impure, their penicillin was a thousand times
stronger than crude penicillin and 10 times more effective than
the strongest sulfanomide.

In May 1940 Florey began the first really crucial test on the
semipurified penicillin. He infected three groups of mice with
three different germs. Some mice in each group were treated
with penicillin, the rest were not. These were part of the "control" group. The penicillin-treated mice got well; the controlled
mice all died.

The results were encouraging, but the team felt they were in
a race against time. The war had steadily worsened, and by June
the Germans seemed on the verge of mounting a massive attack
on England. Florey and Chain were frantic not only to complete
their experiments but to save the mold from destruction if
Oxford was bombed. They went so far as to soak the linings of
their clothes in the brown liquid penicillin. This way, if England
was invaded, one of them might escape to America with enough
spores to start new penicillin cultures.

On July 1 Florey began the final and most critical test. He
injected 50 mice with deadly doses of *Streptococcus* germs. Half
of these mice were then given injections of penicillin every three
hours for 48 hours. The other 25 mice received no penicillin. To
keep on schedule with the injections, Florey and an assistant
slept in the lab, an alarm clock by their side to wake them. At
the end of 16 hours all 25 of the mice not treated with penicillin
were dead. Of the 25 mice treated with penicillin, all but one
recovered. Chain called the results "a miracle."

Chemist Ernst Chain was the man who actually isolated penicillin and succeeded where many before him had failed. When told Fleming was coming to see his results, Chain was surprised to hear that the discoverer of penicillin was still alive. (UPI/Bettmann)

The following month Florey and Chain were ready to share their results with the world. They published a paper on their experiments in *The Lancet*. The article, "Penicillin as a Chemotherapeutic Agent," appeared just before the historic Battle of Britain got underaway.

Here is their conclusion:

> *The results are clear and show that penicillin is active* in vivo *[inside a living organism] against at least three of the organisms inhibited* in vitro *[in a test tube]. It would seem a reasonable hope that all organisms*

inhibited in high dilution in vitro *will also be found to be dealt with* in vivo. *Penicillin does not appear to be related to any chemotherapeutic substance at present in use and is particularly remarkable for its activity against the anaerobic organisms associated with gas-gangrene.*

Among those who read the article was Alexander Fleming, who until then knew nothing about the work at Oxford. Elated, he called Florey immediately and made an appointment to meet him. When Florey told Chain about the call, the 35-year-old biochemist was astonished. He had assumed Fleming had been dead for years!

On the morning of September 2, 1940, Fleming arrived in Oxford, dressed in his customary suit and bow tie. He shook Florey's hand and said in his typically understated style, "I've come to see what you've been doing with my old penicillin." The statement may have irked the Oxford team a bit, but there was much truth to Fleming's claim on the drug. Chain, as has already been mentioned, had actually used an old sample of Fleming's original penicillin mold in his ground-breaking experiments.

Florey took his distinguished visitor on a complete tour of the laboratory, showing him every step in the purifying process. Fleming listened intently, asked some probing questions, but said little more. When he left that afternoon on the train for London, he offered not a word of congratulations. Chain, for one, was not put off by Fleming's diffident manner. "He struck me as a man who had difficulty in expressing himself," he later said, "though he gave the impression of being somebody with a very warm heart doing all he could to appear cold and distant."

Shortly before the Oxford visit, Fleming had received a letter from an old colleague, Dr. E. W. Todd, who now worked at the Belmont Laboratories of the Public Health Department. What he had to say might have pleased Fleming almost as much as the success of Florey's team. "My Dear Flem," Todd wrote, "I was delighted to read in *The Lancet* this morning about penicillin. When can we start production?"

CHAPTER 8 NOTES

p. 55   "You have made something . . ." André Maurois, *The Life of Sir Alexander Fleming*, p. 167.

p. 57   "It was sheer luck . . ." L. J. Ludovici, *Fleming: Discoverer of Penicillin*, p. 172.

p. 60   "The results are clear . . ." Ludovici, *Fleming*, p. 174.

p. 61   "He struck me as a man . . ." Maurois, *The Life of Sir Alexander Fleming*, p. 167.

p. 61   "My Dear Flem . . ." Maurois, *The Life of Sir Alexander Fleming*, p. 168.

9
PENICILLIN GOES TO WAR

The Army is working night and day to the end that not a single American soldier will have to die from an infected wound that might have been healed by penicillin.

—U.S. Surgeon General Norman T. Kirk

Dr. Todd's question to Fleming was a bit premature. Penicillin had worked on mice, but a human being was a very different kind of guinea pig. As the Oxford team well knew, curing a sick human would take 3,000 times the dosage of penicillin used on a mouse. The drug would need to be purer too. Chain went back to work at perfecting the purifying process. He used a vacuum pump to evaporate the water from the penicillin solution and ended up with a yellow powder, the consistency of corn flour. It was purer than the penicillin used on the mice, but it still contained impurities. In this form, the drug would be excreted from the body quickly, making numerous injections necessary. As the team obtained the minute amounts of penicillin, Florey carefully stored them in a refrigerator, waiting patiently for the day when the drug could be tested on a human subject.

That day came in February 1941. An Oxford policeman had cut himself on the corner of the mouth. The cut became infected and he was admitted to Oxford's Radcliffe Infirmary with acute blood poisoning. The man's condition rapidly deteriorated. He was running a high fever, his body was covered with painful sores, and he had difficulty breathing. Sulfonamides were given to him without success. The doctors believed he had only a few days to live.

Florey and Chain were asked to help. Any risk the patient would face from the untested penicillin was offset by his desperate condition. The two men took their entire supply of penicillin from the refrigerator—about one teaspoonful. They injected 200 milligrams into the patient and then repeated the injections with 100 milligrams every three hours.

The reaction was immediate and dramatic. Within 24 hours the man's condition stabilized. In another 24 hours his sores began to disappear and the fever was down. Florey and Chain were elated but also anxious. What would happen when their meager supply of penicillin ran out? In desperation, they recovered some of the penicillin from the patient's urine and used it again. But this only delayed the inevitable. Soon the penicillin was all gone, the injections stopped, and the infection returned. The man died on March 15, 1941.

Florey and Chain were determined to try again. They built up their supply of penicillin and injected several other seriously ill patients. Two, including a youth with an infected hip socket, recovered completely. Florey and Chain had proven that penicillin could kill infectious germs and heal disease in humans as well as in laboratory mice.

To increase their production of penicillin, Florey and Chain now created a minifactory at Oxford. Making penicillin on a larger scale was tricky business. The working area had to be kept as germ-free as possible to prevent contamination of the cultures and the temperature had to be kept cold for the cultures to flourish. Young women, called "penicillin girls," were hired to work in the makeshift factory. They dressed in white overalls, caps and masks to keep the germ count down, and wore woolen scarves and gloves to keep themselves warm in the frigid conditions. Benches and floors were soaked with oil to prevent dust from rising into the air. Germs, carried through the air by dust, could destroy an entire batch of penicillin. Unfortunately, the oil created slippery conditions that caused more than one penicillin girl to take a spill in the line of duty.

The Oxford team used its first store of penicillin to heal the burn wounds of Royal Air Force pilots who survived the devastating Battle of Britain. A small package of the drug was mailed to a bacteriologist working in Egypt with the army's desert troops. A young New Zealand officer serving there was suffering from infections resulting from complicated leg fractures. After being injected with penicillin, the infections in his legs cleared up and he was back on his feet in a month.

But the tiny Oxford factory was incapable of even beginning to meet the enormous demand for penicillin at the battlefront. Huge factories were needed to produce the drug on a massive scale. Ironically, the war, which made the need for penicillin so vital, was the very thing that stopped its immediate production. British business was pushed to the limit to support the war effort. No one had the time, energy, or money necessary to research and manufacture this new and still-experimental drug.

Desperate for help, Florey turned his attention to the United States, which, as of June 1941, had not yet entered the war. With some strains of *Penicillium* in his suitcase, Florey flew to America at the invitation of the Rockefeller Foundation. There he found a willing manufacturer in the mycological section of the North Regional Laboratory in Peoria, Illinois. After much experimentation, the Peoria lab settled on, of all things, corn-steeped liquor as the medium in which to grow the penicillin cultures. The yeast in the alcohol increased and strengthened the yield of penicillin. It proved to be 20 percent more powerful than the penicillin made at Oxford. Yet, however high the quality of the Peoria penicillin, only a small amount was produced. The mold would grow just on the surface of the quart-size containers of culture. The culture needed air to live and couldn't thrive in the liquid itself. The yield from hundreds of these containers was barely enough to keep one patient alive for a day.

But by the time the Japanese attacked Pearl Harbor in December, penicillin production had become a top priority in the United States. Americans were no longer producing it just for British soldiers, but for their own troops as well. The federal government oversaw distribution and the supply of penicillin was strictly rationed, half of it going directly to the army. In a matter of months, American factories across the country were turning out large amounts of penicillin daily. Technicians developed an ingenious method of aerating huge tanks so that the mold could grow in the broth itself, and not only on its surface. Two-story-high vats holding 25,000 gallons of penicillin broth were stirred by rods as big as airplane propellers.

Equally important was the development of a new, faster-growing strain of penicillin. The discovery of this strain is one of the more fascinating stories in penicillin's colorful history. Working in the Peoria plant was Mary Hunt, a dedicated woman whose job was to go to the produce market each day and look for old, rotting fruits and vegetables from which new mold strains could be developed and tested. One day "Moldy Mary," as she was called, came back from her rounds with a rotting cantaloupe melon. The melon produced a strain called *Penicillium chrysogenum* that proved to be 200 times more productive than Fleming's original mold. Most

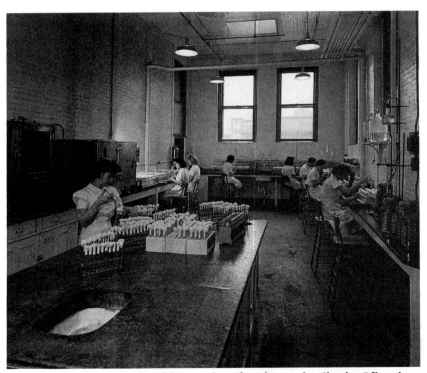

Penicillin is being tested in this American factory run by Charles Pfizer in the mid-1940s. America led the world in penicillin production during World War II. (UPI/Bettmann)

penicillin strains in use today are descended from the mold that grew on this week-old cantaloupe.

The penicillin produced in America was sent to military hospitals for distribution to the battlefront. The results there were truly astonishing. For example, in World War I, 18 percent of the soldiers who contracted pneumonia died. Now—thanks to penicillin—less than 1 percent of pneumonia patients died. And pneumonia was only one of a host of deadly illnesses that penicillin cured. The growing list included strep throat, diphtheria, meningitis, scarlet fever, gas gangrene, syphilis, and gonorrhea.

Despite its growing use in the war, some doctors at the front had a hard time accepting this new drug. Florey, who went to Algiers in North Africa to assist surgeons in using the drug on wounded soldiers, recalled one incident vividly: "I remember one young medical officer looking over my shoulder as I indicated to the surgeon what I wanted him to do. 'It's murder, it's murder,' the voice kept repeating in my ear. It was not pleasant but the patient recovered."

The mounting supply of penicillin was put almost exclusively into the war effort. As yet, it was unavailable to the civilian population in both the United States and Great Britain. But Alexander Fleming would not let this stop him from helping a friend in need. The friend was a director of his brother Robert's optical firm. He lay desperately ill at St. Mary's with an unknown disease, later diagnosed as meningitis.

In August 1942 Fleming called Florey and politely asked if he "could possibly spare a little penicillin." When Fleming explained the situation, Florey immediately turned over his entire supply of penicillin powder to him. Fleming injected the drug into the patient's muscles and noted no improvement in his condition. In desperation, he tried something that had not been attempted before—Fleming injected the penicillin directly into the diseased area—the man's spine.

"Here was a man who seemed to be dying, but who, in a few days, with penicillin treatment, was out of danger," Fleming recalled later. "Such a case makes a great impression on one."

Penicillin's success made a sizable impression on the London *Times* as well, which published a leading article on penicillin on

August 27, 1942. Oddly enough, the newspaper piece made no mention of Fleming, Florey, or Chain. The Old Man of St. Mary's inoculation department was not pleased. Almroth Wright, now 81, wrote a letter to the editor that appeared several days later in the *Times*. " . . . The laurel-wreath for the discovery," Wright wrote, "should be decreed to Professor Alexander Fleming of this research laboratory. For he is the discoverer of penicillin and was the author also of the original suggestion that this substance might prove to have important applications for medicine."

Wright's letter, printed in the country's most reputable newspaper, carried enormous weight. It would start a movement that would lift this little-known research scientist from obscurity to worldwide renown.

A special Penicillin Committee was quickly set up by the minister of supply, Andrew Duncan, to organize the production of penicillin in Great Britain. Fleming, Florey, and Raistrick—the chemist who had failed where Chain had succeeded—served on the committee. With their help, Duncan got five of the country's largest chemical firms to pool their resources and knowledge to increase penicillin production. This might have been difficult to accomplish in peacetime, but under the stress of war, the companies put their natural competitiveness aside for the good of the country.

In November 1944 the world's largest penicillin factory was established in Great Britain. The penicillin produced there was rushed to the battlefront. There it was administered both as a liquid to be injected and as an ointment to be applied directly to the wound's surface. In the famous "D-Day" landing of Allied troops at Normandy on June 6, 1944, 95 percent of soldiers treated with the drug recovered from their wounds.

On the home front, penicillin, while not yet readily available to the general population, was being hailed far and wide as a "wonder drug." Fleming never approved of the term and insisted that penicillin, like any drug, had its limitations. "I have never said that penicillin can cure *everything*," he said. "It is the newspapers that have said that. It does have an extraordinary effect in certain cases of illness, but none in others . . ." He particularly objected to surgeons injecting a dose of penicillin into any patient about to be operated on, as a safety "umbrella." Such practices, he warned, would only build up microbes' resistance to the drug and weaken its effectiveness. Fortunately, this practice was later stopped.

Unlike most drugs, penicillin was not patented by one individual or company. Chemical companies in the United States and Britain worked together, putting cooperative effort above financial gain. However, this didn't stop enterprising businessmen from using the word *penicillin* to sell their products. Soon the stores were flooded with "penicillin" pills, ointments, and eye lotions—none of which contained one grain of penicillin. "I shouldn't wonder if somebody produces a penicillin lipstick," Fleming noted dryly.

But the "product" that was being sold to the public with the greatest enthusiasm was the discoverer himself. Fleming's satisfaction at seeing his discovery fulfilling the great work he envisioned for it must have been tempered by the sudden celebrity now being thrust upon him. Not a charismatic personality like Almroth Wright, Fleming's modesty and singular humility only made him all the more fascinating to the public. All his efforts to downplay his role in penicillin's discovery were in vain. "I didn't do anything," he later insisted. "Nature makes penicillin; I just found it." But nobody wanted to believe him.

As the war ground on, Fleming received an honor he had sought for many years. In 1943 he was finally elected a fellow of the Royal Society. "I can quite honestly say that this is the greatest moment of my life," he told society members who had gathered at St. Mary's to honor him. But the great occasion was not without its moment of terror too. Once more Fleming was forced to face the dreaded speaker's podium.

"They . . . presented me with a very beautiful silver salver," Fleming wrote his old friend artist Ronald Gray. "That was pleasant, but it was not so nice to have to sit on a platform and then make a speech. I hope I did not disgrace myself, but in that matter I am not a good judge . . ."

Terrified as he might have been of public speaking, Fleming showed little fear of other dangers. One night in November 1940, his Chelsea flat was burned by German incendiary bombs during the bombing of London. Fortunately, the Flemings were out at the time. Undaunted, they moved back to Chelsea a few months later. When another bomb exploded nearby, a flying door nearly killed Fleming, who was asleep in bed. When asked about his close call by a laboratory attendant who came by the next day to help clear up, Fleming smiled and said, "When I saw the entire window-frame moving towards me, I decided to get out of bed."

The family next moved outside of London, but Fleming often stayed overnight at St. Mary's so he wouldn't have to lose time from work in commuting. While others took cover in air raid shelters during an enemy attack, Fleming would go up on the roof to watch what he called the "fireworks."

Both doctors and students shared a basement dormitory in the hospital during these difficult days of the war. The camaraderie among them reminded Fleming of his days in the Boulogne hospital ward during World War I. "There was a good deal of the bachelor in him, and he enjoyed the company of men," one colleague later recalled. "Sometimes, when a research-worker was kept late in the laboratory, the door would open, and in would walk the professor—with his neat little bow-tie, and a cigarette dangling from his lips. With an eager and expectant look, he would say: 'What about a pot of beer?' The worker would abandon his microscope and the two of them would go off together to the near-by pub, the Fountains, where they would find other St. Mary's men."

But "Professor Fleming" was about to become "Sir Alexander." In July 1943 Fleming and Florey received one of the highest honors of the kingdom—knighthood. To avoid German bombs, the solemn investiture was held in the basement of Buckingham Palace, where Fleming was formally knighted by King George. "The Lord knows what my new form of address is . . . it will be simply Sir Alexander, I suppose," he mused.

Later in the day, Sir Alexander and Lady Fleming returned to St. Mary's, where he was cruelly snubbed by his old mentor and friend—the same man who had sung his praises in the press. Wright, now semiretired, must have found his former pupil's mounting fame too much to bear and left for home before the staff held a celebration party for him. But this didn't dampen the festivities. For the joyful occasion, the surgeon Sir Zachary Cope wrote a poem, "To Alexander Fleming, Knight."

But the honors were just beginning. At the start of 1945, Fleming was elected president of the newly formed Society of General Microbiology. In his inaugural address he finally found a way to alleviate his fear of speaking—by making light of it. "Other and more distinguished members were asked to assume this presidency, but they were sufficiently strong-minded to refuse it," he said. "But, true to Scottish tradition never to refuse anything, when it came to my turn, I accepted, and I was very pleased until the time came when I received a note from your Secretary saying that I had to deliver the inaugural address . . ."

Fleming's dry wit and self-deprecating manner, once handicaps, now made him immensely likable. The public took this humble little Scotsman to their hearts not just as a great man of medicine but as a human being.

This New York City drugstore manager in 1945 is pleased to be able to offer his customers the new wonder drug, penicillin. With the end of the war, penicillin was available for the first time to the general public, but only with a doctor's prescription. (UPI/Bettmann)

On May 7, 1945, Germany surrendered to the Allied Powers. The terrible war was over in Europe. Britain could now look forward to the peacetime use of penicillin. Medical teams and technicians had the time and energy to improve the antibiotic and make it available to people around the world. The "wonder drug" was about to become the most-heralded medicine in recorded history, and the man who discovered it, a world hero.

CHAPTER 9 NOTES

p. 63 "The Army is working . . ." *Current Biography Yearbook 1944,* p. 210.

p. 67 "I remember one young medical officer . . ." W. A. C. Bullock, *The Man Who Discovered Penicillin: The Life of Sir Alexander Fleming,* p. 97.

p. 67 "Here was a man . . ." André Maurois, *The Life of Sir Alexander Fleming,* p. 181.

p. 68 " . . . The laurel-wreath for the discovery . . ." Maurois, *The Life of Sir Alexander Fleming,* p. 182.

p. 68 "I have never said . . ." Maurois, *The Life of Sir Alexander Fleming,* p. 194.

p. 69 "I shouldn't wonder . . ." Maurois, *The Life of Sir Alexander Fleming,* p. 187.

p. 69 "They . . .presented me with a . . ." Maurois, *The Life of Sir Alexander Fleming,* p. 190.

p. 70 "When I saw . . ." Bullock, *The Man Who Discovered Penicillin,* p. 89.

p. 70 "There was a good deal . . ." Maurois, *The Life of Sir Alexander Fleming,* p. 178.

p. 70 "The Lord knows . . ." L. J. Ludovici, *Fleming: Discoverer of Penicillin,* p. 201.

p. 71 "Other and more distinguished members . . ." Maurois, *The Life of Sir Alexander Fleming,* p. 199.

10

A HOUSEHOLD NAME

*I'm sorry that I can't get used to all this fuss, but I suppose I
have to put up with it.*

—Fleming in a letter to a friend

Although he never fully got used to being a household name at
age 64, Fleming was able to take his newfound fame in stride. The
inner fortitude and calm composure that had seen him through
two world wars now held him in good stead in the face of
"Fleming mania."

This phenomenon reached the peak of absurdity in the notorious Churchill episode. British Prime Minister Winston Churchill had contracted pneumonia in the Middle East and was
cured by a shot of penicillin. Grateful to the man who discovered
the drug, Churchill is reported to have said that this was the
second time that Alexander Fleming had saved his life. Churchill claimed Fleming saved him from drowning years earlier
while on vacation in Scotland. Sir Alec had a good chuckle over
that tale. If it were true, a 14-year-old Churchill would have
been saved from the deep by a 7-year-old Fleming!

He was perceptive enough, however, to see there was a serious
side to all the hoopla. In his travels abroad to promote penicillin,

Fleming realized he was not just a representative of St. Mary's, or the medical profession, but of Great Britain itself. He was a goodwill ambassador for a nation trying to recover from the ravages of war. Although a Scotsman through and through, he symbolized to much of the world the reserved, soft-spoken, quick-witted but basically warm-hearted English gentleman.

His willingness to play the public figure, however, was not all duty to Britannia. Fleming truly enjoyed much of the adulation that came his way, as a child would—relishing all the attention, but never taking it too seriously. As biographer André Maurois observed, "He collected decorations as a schoolboy collects stamps, delighted whenever an especially rare specimen came his way." Few people—in the world of science or any other field of endeavor—have dealt with instant fame with such grace and good humor.

"It is clear to me, that they attach a great deal more importance to penicillin in America than in England," a bemused Fleming said on his second visit to the United State in June 1945. This was another understatement from a master of understatement. Fleming was honored and feted at every stop in his triumphant two-month tour of America. The trip was ostensibly to, in Fleming's words, "see how the baby's growing up" and observe the great advances American companies were making in penicillin production. However, it soon became apparent that it was as much a cross-country celebration of the man who had discovered the "wonder drug" of the century.

Fleming visited and spoke at laboratories, penicillin factories, and colleges and universities. Everywhere he went he was met by crowds of well-wishers and mobs of reporters. Complete strangers would walk up, shake his hand, and thank him profusely for saving their life or that of a family member with his drug.

In New York, Fleming was honored by a banquet at the Waldorf-Astoria and watched a boxing match in Madison Square Garden, one of the few times where he wasn't recognized and hounded by autograph seekers. In Washington, D.C., senators and cabinet members gave him a special Humanitarian Award during a banquet in his honor.

A reporter explained what happened after the dinner:

Fleming examines a slide of a mold culture at the Peoria research laboratory, while Dr. Robert Coghill looks on. Peoria, where penicillin was first manufactured in America, was just one stop on Fleming's triumphant U.S. tour in the summer of 1945. Note the poster on the wall. (UPI/Bettmann)

After dinner and a long evening of speeches and horseplay, the ranking guests departed and the Variety Club people, local and national theatre moguls, were sitting around upstairs having a peaceful nightcap when there was a knock at their door and they opened it to the gentle, unassuming award-winner, Sir Alexander, who stood clutching his plaque under his arm and said shyly that he wanted to tell them all what a good time he had had. He came in and sat around talking with them until five in the morning.

In Chicago, he spoke at a medical conference. And in Oklahoma, of all places, he was serenaded by a band of Scottish bagpipers. One of the tour's highlights was his visit to Harvard University, where he gave the Commencement Day address and picked up an honorary degree of doctor of science.

In his address, he gave the graduates some good advice on success and how to prepare for it:

> . . . *If I might offer advice to the young laboratory worker, it would be this—never to neglect an extraordinary appearance or happening. It may be—usually is, in fact—a false alarm which leads to nothing, but it may on the other hand be the clue provided by fate to lead you to some important advance. But I warn you of the danger of first sitting and waiting till chance offers something. We must work, and work hard. We must know our subject. We must master all the technicalities of our craft. Pasteur's often quoted dictum that Fortune favors the prepared mind is undoubtedly true, for the unprepared mind cannot see the outstretched hand of opportunity.*
>
> *This is then nothing new in my advice to the young. Work hard, work well, do not clutter up the mind too much with precedents, and be prepared to accept such good fortune as the gods offer . . .*

Fleming's "good fortune" had its downside. Reporters plagued him wherever he went, badgering him with endless questions about his work and personal life. He rarely lost his good humor in the face of the ever-present press, however. Once, when going down to breakfast from his hotel room, an American reporter asked him, in all seriousness, "What does a great scientist think about when he is going in to breakfast?"

The great scientist looked at the man with feigned surprise. "It's curious you should ask me that," he replied solemnly. "It so happens that I am thinking about something rather special."

"What?" asked the reporter, pencil to pad.

"Well, I was wondering whether I should have one egg or two," he replied.

After heading north to Canada and touring its penicillin plants, Fleming returned home in August to find another invitation waiting for him. He was to address the French Academy of Medicine in Paris and receive France's highest award, the Legion of Honor. In his address he tried once again to play down his role in penicillin's success. "I have been accused of having invented penicillin," he told his distinguished audience. "No man could *invent* penicillin, for it has been produced from time immemorial by a certain mold."

Such modesty didn't prevent author Georges Duhamel from telling Fleming later in a cafe, "You, sir, have gone a step farther than Pasteur."

Fleming shook his white head. "But for Pasteur," he protested, "I should be nothing!"

On October 25, he received a telegram from Stockholm, Sweden, informing him that he been awarded the 1945 Nobel Prize for Medicine along with Ernst Chain and Sir Howard Florey. This honor, the highest of its kind in the world, included a cash award of £7,500 and worldwide prestige.*

Although the prize for penicillin was a three-way split, all the attention in England was focused on Fleming. There were several reasons for this. First, Fleming was a native son, while both Florey and Chain were immigrants. Second, the other two men were part of a research team and did not capture the public imagination as Fleming, the lone scientist working in his dingy lab, did and still does. Finally, Fleming was indeed the man who discovered penicillin. Without his contribution, Chain and Florey could have done nothing. On the other hand, their work was just as vital. Without their breakthrough, penicillin's potential might have remained a secret for years and Fleming might have gone to his grave in obscurity. It should be noted that Fleming himself was always generous in sharing credit with the Oxford team. If they were pushed out of the limelight, it was largely the work of other hands.

---

* The previous year a rumor had spread that Fleming would win the prize, but it went instead to two Americans, Joseph Erlanger and Herbert Gasser, for their pioneering work in neurophysiology.

On December 6, Fleming flew to Stockholm for the Nobel presentations. In a letter to his friend John Cameron, he described the auspicious occasion:

> . . . with fanfares of trumpets we were ushered on to a platform and sitting before us were the whole of the Royal Family and thousands of audience. Then trumpets, orchestra, singing, speeches and receiving our awards from the King. After the reward a banquet of about 700 where I sat beside the Crown Princess . . . then after the banquet we adjourned to a students' sing-song and dance. Home at 3 a.m. . . .

The next day he delivered his official lecture and then had dinner with the king of Sweden in his palace. Afterward, he drank Swedish beer at the hotel bar with some of his fellow recipients. "Among us there was an Argentine woman poet [actually, Chilean Gabriela Mistral] who got a Nobel Prize but could not stand up to the drink," he wrote.

The same year, St. Mary's honored its Nobel Prize-winning bacteriologist by renaming the new Institute of Microbiology the Wright-Fleming Institute. Wright finally retired in 1946 and Fleming became the principal, or head, administrator. It was not a position he relished. He was a research scientist and not an administrator. The politics that went with the position abhorred him.

October 26, 1946 was a special day in the life of the great man. He visited his hometown of Darvel with Sareen and Robert at his side. The town presented its famous son with an illustrated scroll. Fleming joked that an amazing number of townspeople claimed to have been at school with him. However, it was clear the occasion moved him deeply, as can be seen from these words in his address:

> I have not been in this countryside for many years. The people change but the country is the same. The same pools are in the burn, and the country is just the same; and I have no doubt the same trout we guddled as boys are under the same stones.

He ended his speech by saying:

Fleming (second from left) poses after receiving the 1945 Nobel Prize for Medicine in Stockholm, Sweden. The other recipients are, from the left, Artturi Virtanen (Chemistry), Ernst Chain (co-winner, Medicine), Gabriela Mistral (Literature), and Howard Florey (co-winner, Medicine).
(UPI/Bettmann)

The object of research is the advancement not of the investigator but of knowledge . . . It is the glory of a good bit of work that it opens the way to better things and thus rapidly leads to its own eclipse.

Between his many trips, Fleming continued to work in the lab, and wrote scientific articles on the uses of penicillin for such journals as *The Lancet* and the *British Medical Journal.* Despite his worldwide fame, he remained the same old Flem to his colleagues. His door was always open to anyone who wanted to pop in and see what he was up to. One of these people was an attractive 34-year-old Greek bacteriologist, Amalia Voureka, who went to St. Mary's in October 1946 as a researcher. Fleming was impressed by her dedication and outgoing personality and offered her a position where she could work with him. When the grant that financed Dr. Voureka's position ran out, Fleming helped her obtain a research scholarship that was endowed by one of his American admirers.

On April 30, 1947, Almroth Wright died at age 87. It was a heavy blow to Fleming. Wright had been his mentor since he first entered the medical field nearly half a century earlier. He had been his teacher, his guide, and his friend. They were very different people, but they had shared a common vision. Both men believed that the body's natural defenses could cure nearly any disease or illness if given a little help. Fleming had carried that vision into a new era of medicine. Penicillin was the first, and perhaps the greatest, of the antibiotics. Wright had lived to see the dawn of that age. Now it was up to Fleming to carry on the work alone.

He would continue to do valid work with penicillin and other substances, but his importance as a public figure and promoter of penicillin would now overshadow his work in the laboratory. Fleming's travels and lectures around the world kept penicillin research moving forward and gave people something positive to believe in after six years of a destructive world war.

In May 1948, he and Sareen were invited to Madrid, Spain. The Spanish people took Fleming to their hearts, kneeling before him and kissing his hand in gratitude for penicillin. He went to the bullfight where he upstaged the matadors and signed countless autographs. But then the joyous trip was marred by unexpected sadness. Sareen collapsed and had to return to England. Since the war her boundless energy had been waning. Her husband's fame and their hectic schedule, on top of volunteer work she had done during the war, had worn down her resistance. After Spain, she would no longer accompany him on his trips.

Fleming himself, at 67, was as fit as ever. He kept up a pace that would exhaust men half his age. By the end of his life he had traveled the world to receive a total of 25 honorary degrees, 26 medals, 18 prizes, 13 decorations, and 89 honorary memberships to societies and academies. In two days in 1945 he received three honorary degrees in Belgium, setting some kind of a record.

In June 1949, he was made a member of the Pontifical Academy of Science in Rome and received a special audience with the pope. "He is a nice little man," Fleming later told a friend.

"He sat on one side of the fireplace, and I sat on the other, and we talked a bit. Then he pulled this [papal medal] out of his pocket and gave it to me. Not to be outdone, I gave him one of mine."

The *Penicillium* medallion he gave the pope was, like his germ paintings, Fleming's own unique and original design. He would grow the organism on a paper disk, fix it with formalin, and mount it between glass sheets. Then he would enclose the glass in gold or a tortoise-shell rim and give it to visitors and guests as gifts. The

Fleming meets Pope Pius XII at the Vatican during an international congress of physicians. At an earlier meeting, he described the Holy Father as "a nice little man." The pope gave Fleming a papal medal and Fleming gave him one of his own unique *"Penicillium* medallions." (UPI/Bettmann)

medallion he gave to the pope is today among the Vatican's precious treasures.

Shortly after, Fleming traveled to Oklahoma City, where he gave one of his finest speeches at the inauguration of the "Oklahoma Foundation" for medical research. He voiced his concern over the latest medical technology and found it no substitute for the scientist's best tool—an inquiring mind.

> If a worker who has been used to an ordinary laboratory is transplanted to a marble palace, one of two things will happen: either he will conquer the marble palace, or the marble palace will conquer him. If he wins, the palace becomes a workshop and takes on the appearance of an ordinary laboratory. If the palace wins, then he is lost . . . My own laboratory has been described in an American paper as looking like "the back-room of an old-fashioned drug-store"—but I would not have exchanged it for the largest and most luxurious of installations . . . I have known research-workers reduced to impotence by apparatus so fine and elaborate that they spent all their time playing with a plethora of ingenious mechanical devices. The machine conquered the man, instead of the man conquering the machine.

After the speech, a woman asked him to what he attributed his success. He replied, "I can only suppose that God wanted penicillin, and that that was His reason for creating Alexander Fleming."

But all the adulation and honors could not wipe out one sad, inevitable fact—Sareen was dying. She was gravely ill with what doctors now believe was Parkinson's disease, a degenerative illness that attacks the nervous system. She was hospitalized at St. Mary's and then, as her condition worsened, moved to a nursing home. A woman friend recalled talking to Fleming about Sareen's illness: "I shall never forget the look on his face when he said, 'And the most horrible thing about it is that penicillin can do nothing for her . . . When John died* it had not been perfected; now it has, but is useless in Sareen's case.'"

She died on October 28, 1949. Fleming's constant companion and closest confidante of 34 years was gone. "My life is broken," he told a friend. And for a while it indeed seemed so. For the first

---

* His brother John died of pneumonia in 1937.

time in his many years at St. Mary's, his door was shut to visitors. His son Robert, now a doctor in his own right, was a comfort to him, but when Robert went into the army in 1951, he was alone again. He saw his younger brother Robert and his wife occasionally on weekends, but his only regular companion was John's widow, Sareen's sister Elizabeth, who had moved into the London house after her husband's death. Elizabeth's melancholic state only deepened Fleming's own sense of loss. But life was not through with Alexander Fleming. Just when all the joy seemed drained from his life, it returned, from a most unexpected source.

CHAPTER 10 NOTES

p. 73   "I'm sorry that I can't get used to . . ." André Maurois, *The Life of Sir Alexander Fleming*, p. 209.

p. 74   "He collected decorations . . ." Maurois, *The Life of Sir Alexander Fleming*, p. 219.

p. 74   "It is clear to me . . ." Maurois, *The Life of Sir Alexander Fleming*, p. 201.

p. 75–76 "After dinner and a long evening . . ." L. J. Ludovici, *Fleming: Discoverer of Penicillin*, p. 205.

p. 76   " . . . If I might offer advice . . ." Maurois, *The Life of Sir Alexander Fleming*, p. 204.

p. 76   "What does a great scientist . . ." Maurois, *The Life of Sir Alexander Fleming*, pp. 202–203.

p. 77   "I have been accused . . ." Maurois, *The Life of Sir Alexander Fleming*, p. 207.

p. 77   "You, sir, have gone a step farther . . ." Maurois, *The Life of Sir Alexander Fleming*, p. 208.

p. 78   " . . . with fanfares of trumpets . . ." Maurois, *The Life of Sir Alexander Fleming*, p. 212.

p. 78   "I have not been in this countryside . . ." John Rowland, *The Penicillin Man*, pp. 146–147.

p. 80   "He is a nice little man . . ." Gwyn Macfarlane, *Alexander Fleming: The Man and the Myth*, p. 231.

p. 82   "If a worker who has . . ." Maurois, *The Life of Sir Alexander Fleming*, pp. 232–233.

p. 82   "I can only suppose . . ." Maurois, *The Life of Sir Alexander Fleming*, p. 233.

p. 82   "I shall never forget . . ." Maurois, *The Life of Sir Alexander Fleming*, pp. 233-234.

11

A SECOND CHANCE AT HAPPINESS

"You mustn't die. What would your husband do without you?"
"Oh, he'll marry again, but whoever it is, she'll have to do the proposing!"

—exchange between Sareen Fleming and a close friend
shortly before her death

On his 70th birthday, in August 1951, Fleming was asked what was his formula for a happy old age. "Keep on working" was his succinct reply. And he did. Work in the laboratory gradually brought him out of the depression caused by Sareen's death. And his most devoted and constant co-worker now was Amalia Voureka. The young woman and her dedication to bacteriology might well have reminded Fleming of himself as a younger man. Her freshness, pleasing personality and unflagging energy worked like a tonic on the aging widower.

Together they studied the bacillus *Proteus vulgaris* and the astonishing effect penicillin had on it. The drug caused dramatic changes in a culture of the microbes. The microbes' long, leggy flagella—lashlike appendages that help the proteus move about—were normally invisible. Under the influence of the penicillin, they suddenly became visible under a microscope. One variety of proteus appeared to have flagella that resembled large wings. The wings moved wildly for a few seconds as the proteus tried vainly to get out of a corner of the culture dish and then abruptly stopped. Amalia quickly found a way to start it moving again. She moved the mirror that refracted light onto the microbe. The light served as a stimulus that set the wings beating again. Fleming was delighted with her success and spent long hours studying the proteus's movements and recording them.

In a memo to a colleague he wrote:

> *They [the proteus] roll themselves up like watch-springs, and go round and round like Catherine-wheels* all day long in the same field of the microscope. We can time their movements, stop them, start them, and observe how their flagella move. They respond beautifully to stimuli, and I was beginning to believe that even a lowly bacterium has some primitive nervous system.*

He collaborated with Amalia on a paper about the bacillus that was published in the *Journal of General Microbiology*. It was typical of his generous nature that Fleming shared credit on articles with Amalia and several other younger colleagues. By doing this, he hoped to give them the exposure in the scientific community that he no longer needed.

Gradually Amalia became more and more indispensable to her mentor. An accomplished linguist, she served as his interpreter when non-English speaking foreign guests visited the laboratory. She also translated his lectures given abroad for publication. They began seeing each other socially as well as at work. Amalia was Fleming's escort to some of the many social functions he was required to attend. He even invited her down to the Dhoon one August weekend and was delighted to find she loved the quiet refuge from the bustling city as much as he did.

The Dhoon had fallen into serious disrepair during the war years. It had been damaged by German bombs and the exhausting work of putting it back in shape had undoubtedly contributed to Sareen's last illness. Fleming had set up a little lab for himself there so he could work and not have to rush back to London after the weekend. On her visit, Amalia cleaned up the lab and worked there with him. The weekend stretched into a week. They fished, went antique hunting, and enjoyed the peacefulness of nature. But finally the time came for Amalia to leave.

---

* A kind of fireworks that revolves when lit, like a pinwheel.

Shortly after, Fleming wrote her the following note:

My dear Amalie,

I hope that is the way to spell your name, but am not sure . . . we are all lonely since you left—you cheered us all up—and I have no one to help me with my nettle-cutting.

You found that the little laboratory suited you, so you had better collect some cultures and bring them down.

Be good to the mice.

Yours, A. F.

In her written reply she admitted she had "massacred" 18 mice in an experiment and gently corrected him on the spelling of her name.

Their warm relationship continued to grow. When an opportunity arose for Amalia to return to her native Greece and take a good position at a hospital, Fleming was disappointed. Yet he did not attempt to stop her from leaving. Although he would miss her keenly, he didn't want to stand in the way of her career. She left for Greece in December 1951, leaving behind a lonely, old man. "I cross the park alone now; no one to talk to me," he wrote her in a letter. "We miss you all the time."

But constant travel and seemingly endless honors helped to fill the emptiness in his life. He was named to a UNESCO (United Nations Educational, Scientific, and Cultural Organization) commission where his job was to organize medical conferences. Then he was elected rector of Edinburgh University in his native Scotland. This was an appointment particularly dear to Fleming's heart because the honorary post was elected not by the administration or teaching staff, but by the students.

There were eight candidates for the rectorship that year, including the popular Asian ruler the Aga Khan, but Fleming beat them all. The students loved his wit, his playfulness, and his sincere humility. In his speech on his installation at Edinburgh, he attributed his great success to "hard work, careful observation, clear thinking, enthusiasm and a spot of luck." Then he spoke about a subject he often touched on in his speeches, teamwork. He gave full credit to the Oxford team for succeeding in isolating penicillin, where he, working alone, had failed. But then he added: "It is the lone worker who makes the first advance in a subject: the details may be worked out by a team, but the prime idea is due to the enterprise, thought and perception of an individual." He pointed out that if he had been part of a team at St. Mary's, "it is likely that I would have had to play for the team and so neglect this chance occurrence which had nothing whatever to do with the problems in hand."

After the ceremony ended, the students hoisted their new rector on their shoulders and carried him outside to a formal tea. In a letter to a friend, Fleming commented, "It was a very exciting experience and after 70 years didn't want too much excitement . . ."

But he hardly seemed ready for the easy chair. When he heard a World Medical Association meeting was being held in Athens, Greece in October 1952, Fleming immediately offered to be a representative, claiming he had "interests in Athens."

Amalia was elated to see her old boss and dear friend and acted as his guide and interpreter for his entire stay in Greece. He received a glorious reception in the land of Hippocrates, the father of medicine. He was given an olive branch from the tree under which the great philosopher Plato supposedly taught his pupils. The city of Athens gave him two medals of honor. With Amalia by his side, he had a memorable time, but the days flew and soon it was time to depart.

On the last night of his stay, Amalia invited him to her house for dinner. There was an unspoken sadness in the air for both of them that evening. As Amalia related years later to André Maurois, Fleming muttered something as he was about to leave that she didn't hear.

"You haven't answered me," he said a moment later.

"Did you say anything?" she asked, startled.

"I asked you to marry me," came the reply.

Amalia thought a long moment and then without further hesitation said yes.

Yet for two very busy people even marriage had to wait. They set the date for the wedding for the following April, after a trip Fleming had planned to India. He returned home as happy and excited as a schoolboy. He wrote Amalia every day and looked

In 1952, Fleming was elected rector of Edinburgh University by its students. Here the students show their enthusiasm for their countryman by carrying him to tea on their shoulders after his installation. Fleming collected over 180 honors in the last decade of his life. (New York Public Library Picture Collection)

forward to India with eager anticipation, knowing he would be seeing her soon after. On his trip he participated in a walking race, joined in a leopard hunt, and haunted the bazaars buying saris and jewelry for Amalia. (As closed-lipped as ever about his private life, he told inquisitive friends the gifts were for his sister.)

On April 9, 1953, Alec and Amalia were married in a civil ceremony at the Chelsea Registry Office. Their friends and family joined them at a religious ceremony later that day at a Greek church, from which they went directly to Cuba for their honeymoon. From Cuba, the newlyweds traveled to America, where they were barraged with interviews for the press, radio, and television.

Despite the 32-year age difference, Fleming's second marriage was as happy and contented as his first. On their return to London, the couple spent every night either dining out or entertaining friends at their Chelsea home. There was no question that this older husband could keep up with his young wife.

The first sign of change occurred in October. Fleming was scheduled to give a speech in Nice, France. Two days before the event, he developed pneumonia. His doctor gave him an injec-

Fleming poses for a picture with his second wife, Amalia, on their wedding day in 1953. Despite the great difference in their ages, it was a happy marriage, cut short by Fleming's death two years later.
(UPI/Bettmann)

tion of penicillin and Fleming fully recovered. "I had no idea it was so good!" he exclaimed. While he recuperated at home, Amalia delivered his speech in Nice, further proof of the close partnership in their marriage. The pneumonia did have one positive side effect. It convinced him to give up his lifelong smoking habit. He had once smoked as many as 60 cigarettes a day.

Meanwhile, his fame continued to grow. The writer L. J. Ludovici wanted to write his biography. Fleming cooperated, although he did so under the impression the book wouldn't be published until after his death. When *Fleming, Discoverer of Penicillin* came out in 1953, the ever-modest Fleming was taken aback but pleased and flattered by the accurate and positive portrait of his life. However, he flatly refused when a Hollywood producer approached him about making a movie of his life. "It might be all right after I am dead," he said. "Now, I'm still trying to do a job of work."

Oddly enough, he did consent to have himself represented in a stained-glass window in St. James Church in Paddington. When someone pointed out that it was strange to have a memorial window made when you were still alive, Fleming, with good humor, replied that time would soon set that right.

To make better use of the time he had left, he resigned as principal of the Wright-Fleming Institute in January 1955. The burden of administration was finally lifted from his shoulders, and he was free to devote himself exclusively to the laboratory research that was his first love. At a dinner given on his retirement at St. Mary's, he told his colleagues, "This is not goodbye. I shall be here for years, so don't think you are getting rid of me."

But for once he had been too optimistic. Only a month later he came down with a bad case of gastric flu. "From that moment, a change came over him," recalled Amalia. "He seemed to be utterly exhausted." The years of constant traveling and speech making to promote penicillin had finally caught up with him. But he refused to cut back on his hectic schedule.

Friday, March 11, 1955 started out as a normal day. Fleming was scheduled that evening to have dinner with Eleanor Roosevelt and the actor Douglas Fairbanks, Jr. He awoke feeling fit but came out of the bathroom looking weak and pale. Amalia was concerned and immediately called his doctor. Fleming, ever thinking of others before himself, insisted the doctor see his other patients first before coming round to have a look at him. Upon hanging up the phone, he calmed Amalia's fears, insisting it was his stomach that was the problem and not his heart. As they quietly talked, he suddenly slumped forward. Alexander Fleming, at age 73, was dead of a massive heart attack.

The world that had celebrated his life and work mourned his passing with equal fervor. In Barcelona, Spain, flower-sellers decorated a tablet commemorating his visit there with bright flowers. In Greece, the flags were flown at half-mast, leading two travelers to ask an old man near Delphi what had happened to cause such widespread grief. "Do you not know," the old man said, "that Fleming is dead?"

His funeral in London was a national event. The burial took place at the crypt of Saint Paul's Cathedral—an honor reserved for only the greatest of Englishmen. According to his wishes, his body was cremated and the ashes interred under a flagstone marked simply "A. F." Above it, on a tablet of marble from Greece, was carved the thistle, the national symbol of Scotland, and a lily, the emblem of St. Mary's Hospital.

The ushers at the service were the people who had worked alongside him—the students and nurses of St. Mary's. Charles Pannett, his friend since their student days at St. Mary's, delivered the funeral ovation.

He recalled his first meeting with Fleming:

> *He was a little older and more mature than the rest of us, a quiet man with alert, blue, penetrating, resolute eyes . . . For the first few years we were rivals but afterwards our paths diverged, yet never was this band of friendship strained, for Fleming had that steadiness and steadfastness of character that gave the quality of security to a friendship which lasted unsullied until his death. This constancy of his was outstanding and inspired a confidence in his friends and companions which was never misplaced . . .*

Then he talked about an aspect of his friend's life that many were not aware of:

Fleming's coffin is carried into St. Paul's Cathedral where his ashes are interred in the crypt that houses the remains of many other distinguished Britons. (New York Public Library Picture Collection)

I shall not speak of his hopes, his strivings, his disappointments and frustration . . . Every great scientist knows these and Fleming experienced them in full measure . . . but there is a remarkable aspect of Fleming's life which is not so widely known. Looking back on his career, we find woven into the web of his life a number of apparently irrelevant chance events without one of which it would probably not have reached its climax. There were so many of these events, and they were all so purposive that we feel driven to deny their being due to mere chance . . .

His choice of a profession, his selection of a medical school, his deviation into bacteriology, his meeting with Almroth Wright, the nature of the work he did with him, the chance drop of a tear, the chance fall of a mold, all these events were surely not due to mere chance. We can almost see the finger of God pointed to the direction his career should take at every turn.

At another point in his eulogy, Pannett paid his old friend the ultimate honor. "By his work he has saved more lives and relieved more suffering than any other living man, perhaps more than any man who has ever lived." No one then, and few now, would attempt to challenge this statement.

CHAPTER 11 NOTES

p. 85   "You mustn't die . . ." André Maurois, *The Life of Sir Alexander Fleming*, p. 99.

p. 86   "They roll themselves up . . ." Maurois, *The Life of Sir Alexander Fleming*, p. 236.

p. 87   "May dear Amalie . . ." Maurois, *The Life of Sir Alexander Fleming*, p. 242.

p. 87   "I cross the park alone . . ." Maurois, *The Life of Sir Alexander Fleming*, p. 245.

p. 88   "It is the lone worker . . ." Maurois, *The Life of Sir Alexander Fleming*, p. 251.

p. 88   "It was a very exciting experience . . ." Maurois, *The Life of Sir Alexander Fleming*, p. 249.

p. 88   "You haven't answered . . ." Maurois, *The Life of Sir Alexander Fleming*, p. 255.

p. 91   "It might be all right . . ." Gywn Macfarlane, *Alexander Fleming: The Man and the Myth*, p. 239.

p. 91   "This is not goodbye . . ." Maurois, *The Life of Sir Alexander Fleming*, p. 269.

p. 91   "From that moment . . ." Maurois, *The Life of Sir Alexander Fleming*, p. 269.

p. 92   "Do you not know . . ." W. A. C. Bullock, *The Man Who Discovered Penicillin: The Life of Sir Alexander Fleming*, p. 114.

p. 92   "He was a little older . . ." Maurois, *The Life of Sir Alexander Fleming*, pp. 274–275.

12

THE ANTIBIOTIC AGE

The extraordinary merit of penicillin has trained the searchlight on a new field . . . What now remains is the synthesis of penicillin, and this has much wider significance than just an increase in production. The chemists will fasten on the molecule and modify it, as they have done with the sulfanilamide molecule in the last five years, so that derivatives of penicillin will appear more powerful, or with wider applications, and diseases now untouched will be conquered.

—Alexander Fleming in his acceptance speech on receiving the Award of Distinction from the American Pharmaceutical Manufactures Association in December 1943

Penicillin did not die with Alexander Fleming. In the decades following his death it flourished, saving millions of lives that would have perished without it. In the late 1950s, chemists were busy working on new varieties of the antibiotic that would super-cede penicillin G, the most effective and common penicillin used in Fleming's day. Penicillin G, for all its good points, had its problems as a germ fighter. It did not kill certain types of deadly bacteria, and many of the bacteria it did kill eventually built up resistance to it. Penicillin G was also ineffective when take orally because stomach acids destroyed it before it could reach the bloodstream.

The solution was the development of semisynthetic penicil-lins—a combination of natural substances and artificially made chemicals. These new varieties, including Ampicillin and Amoicillin, are commonly used today in treating throat and ear infections in children and urinary tract infections in adults.

Other problems with penicillin have developed since the death of its discoverer that have not been so easily remedied. For the great majority of patients who were given the drug, there were no negative side effects. But as time went on, it became apparent that a sizable portion of the population—as high as 10 percent—was allergic to penicillin. Allergic reactions are usually mild, including rashes and fever. But in some cases reactions can be life-threatening, such as shock and difficulty in breathing. A sobering statistic in penicillin's history was the first death reported from taking the drug after 100 million doses were administered. Today, before prescribing penicillin, most physicians will ask if the patient has ever had an allergic reaction to the drug. If so, often another antibiotic can be substituted.

The other modern-day problem with penicillin, as well as the other antibiotics developed in its wake, is one that Fleming foresaw years earlier—the development of penicillin-resistant strains of microbes. While billions of bacteria are destroyed when attacked by penicillin, a very few with strong resistance survive. These survivors, which have no competition from other bacteria, multiply. The new bacteria created is even more resistant. Eventually this process results in a whole new strain of extremely resistant bacteria.

The growth of these strains was well underway, even as penicillin was earning its reputation as a "miracle drug." In the late 1940s, 85 percent of staphylococci infections were easily cured with regular doses of penicillin. But by the early 1950s, up to 80 percent of these same germs were highly resistant to the drug.

The war against bacteria, which one writer has compared to the nuclear arms race, has continued to escalate in recent years. More potent antibiotics are developed to combat more resilient bacteria, which in turn become resistant to the antibiotics, leading to the development of stronger antibiotics, and so on. In the early 1980s, one drug company felt it had finally created a group of antibiotics so powerful that even the most resistant of bacteria would be destroyed by it for years to come. One of these superdrugs was an

The penicillin mold *Penicillium notatum* is seen growing in flasks in a medical drug manufacturing laboratory. Chemists have produced a number of stronger semisynthetic strains of penicillin in the years since Fleming's death. (UPI/Bettmann)

advanced form of penicillin that broke down more slowly in the human body, thus giving the drug a longer time to kill bacteria. But it quickly became apparent that the superdrugs were no match for the adaptable bacteria. As early as 1983, some germs were found to be building up an effective resistance to them.

The solution to this problem was first voiced years before by Fleming—use antibiotics only when they are necessary to combat infection. Fleming's words of warning had been long forgotten in the decades since his death. One recent report estimates that up to 60 percent of antibiotic usage is inappropriate or unnecessary. Many doctors prescribe antibiotics for colds and viruses where they do little good and much potential harm. Viruses are immune to most drugs, including antibiotics. Only virus symptoms, such as a high fever, can be treated. The drug leaves the virus unaffected, but it kills nonresistant bacteria, encouraging the growth and spread of the resistant bacteria.

As Fleming himself would have been the first to admit, the "battle against the bug" may never end in a decisive victory. However, the most deadly bacteria can be contained with sensible use of antibiotics and the continued development of more effective drugs. This is the challenge that faces today's bacteriologists.

How will history judge the achievements of Alexander Fleming? Although he was lauded in his lifetime as the discoverer of penicillin, Fleming himself felt his most enduring achievement was the method of fighting germs that penicillin exemplified. He proved that substances found in nature—such as antibiotics—were the best defense against bacteria. They could be enhanced by human technological skills but never replaced by them. Time has proven him correct.

Penicillin was followed by a host of other natural antibiotics, discovered in molds and bacteria, including streptomycin, tetra-cycline, vancomycin and chloramphenicol. Of the over 60 kinds of antibiotics in use today, most are useful in fighting bacterial infections. A few are used to fight harmful protozoa and fungi. Some antibiotics not only combat disease in humans but in ani-mals as well, particularly such farm animals as cows, sheep, and pigs. They also control bacteria that are harmful to grains and fruit. Antibiotics are used in small amounts by farmers to stimulate livestock growth and by food companies as a preservative.

As important as Fleming's discovery of penicillin was, it has unfairly overshadowed his admirable work with war wounds in World War I and his subsequent discovery of lysozyme. Some scientists today even see these accomplishments as more outstand-ing than penicillin. Penicillin, they argue, owed as much to Florey and Chain as it did to Fleming, while his earlier discoveries were more completely his own.

In his ground-breaking biography, *Alexander Fleming: The Man and the Myth*, author Gwyn Macfarlane takes Fleming to task for not doing more to develop penicillin before the Oxford's team success. He also criticizes Fleming for not doing more serious work on penicillin after the drug was purified. While admiring

Fleming's creative approach to science, Macfarlane claims that Fleming "had no original attitude to research or teaching that would inspire" the creation of a school of scientific thought or method. Yet when we review Almroth Wright's career, the pitfalls of such "a school of thought" with its overbearing and dogmatic approach are clear. Perhaps Fleming's more intuitive and individual approach to research and discovery was just as influential and inspiring to scientists who followed him as any school could be.

It is natural today to look back at the adulation Fleming received in the last decade of his life and think it excessive. But after the megalomania of such world figures as Hitler, Stalin, and Mussolini, who came close to destroying Europe and its civilization, people needed a new kind of hero to look to. This humble man of science, who worked to save human life, not destroy it, filled that role perfectly.

Fleming reluctantly accepted the world's fame, but he made no fortune from it. Penicillin did not make him rich and he never expected it to. When a group of American penicillin manufacturers gratefully awarded him $100,000 during his 1945 tour of their country, he agreed to accept it, but on the understanding that it would be used only for further research at St. Mary's.

The international acclaim he received turned the humble researcher into a public figure and transformed the awkward public speaker into a spokesperson of grace and wit. Fleming not only discovered penicillin, but became its greatest advocate, helping to usher in the modern age of antibiotics. He was also a plain and good man who was an inspiring role model for millions in an increasingly complicated world. In our own day of corporate technology and declining values, he is no less an inspiration.

Perhaps the best evaluation of Alexander Fleming was made by Fleming himself in a speech he gave at Louvain, Belgium in 1945:

> *My occupation is a simple one. I play with microbes. There are, of course, many rules in this play, and a certain amount of knowledge is required before you can fully enjoy the game, but when you have acquired knowledge and experience, it is very pleasant to break the rules and to be able to find something that nobody had thought of . . .*

This bust of Fleming stands in the main square of his hometown of Darvel, Scotland. It is just one of the many memorials to the great bacteriologist. A crater on the moon has even been named in his honor.
(author's photo)

CHAPTER 12 NOTES

p. 95   "The extraordinary merit of penicillin . . ." *Current Biography Yearbook 1944*, p. 210.

p. 99   "had no original attitude . . ." Gwyn Macfarlane, *Alexander Fleming: The Man and the Myth,* p. 272.

p. 99   "My occupation is a simple one . . ." André Maurois, *The Life of Sir Alexander Fleming*, p. 211.

GLOSSARY

agar: a jellylike substance extracted from seaweed that is used in making bacteria cultures.

antibiotic: a natural substance produced by a living organism, such as a fungus or bacterium, that destroys or weakens germs.

antibodies: proteins produced in the blood or bodily tissues that destroy bacteria and other foreign germs or neutralize their poisons.

antiseptic: a chemical substance that kills or prevents the growth of infectious germs.

bacillus: name of a group of rod-shaped bacteria that form spores.

bacteria: microscopic single-celled organisms that are rodlike, spherical, or spiral in shape. Some cause disease, others are beneficial.

bacteriologist: a scientist who studies bacteria, looking for new ways to combat the diseases they cause.

biochemist: a scientist who studies the chemical processes of living things.

broth: a nutritive soup in which scientists can grow organisms and observe them.

chemotherapy: the treatment of disease by the use of specific chemicals that attack a particular type of disease-producing germ.

control group: a group used as a standard of comparison for testing the results of a laboratory experiment performed on a similar group that is treated differently.

culture: a growth of bacteria specially nurtured for scientific study.

enzyme: a chemical substance produced in the body that works to change other chemicals or begin or speed up a reaction without being changed itself.

immune system: a system of antibodies and white blood cells that attack and destroy germs and other harmful matter that enter the body.

infection: a disease caused by germs or viruses.

inoculation: the process of infecting a person with weakened or dead disease germs to raise the body's defenses in order to prevent that person from getting the disease.

leukocytes: white bloods cells, the body's main defense against invading germs.

lysozyme: a natural substance, discovered by Alexander Fleming in 1922, that is produced by human, animal, and plant life, and kills germs or prevents their growth.

microbes: harmful microorganisms that cause disease; germs.

mold: a fungus growth that thrives on vegetable or animal matter decaying in a warm, moist place.

mucus: a slimy substance produced by the mucous membrances of the nose and throat.

opsonic index: the ratio of the number of bacteria eaten by phagocytes treated with opsonin, a substance in blood serum that makes microbes more appetizing to phagocytes, to the number eaten in normal, untreated blood.

pathology: the scientific study of disease and its causes.

penicillin: a powerful antibiotic produced by molds, first discovered by Alexander Fleming in 1928 and isolated by Howard Florey and Ernst Chain in 1940.

Penicillium: a category of fungus, some types of which produce penicillin.

Petri dish: a shallow, round glass or plastic dish used in preparing bacteria cultures.

phagocytes: special kinds of white blood cells that attack and digest invading bacteria and other foreign bodies.

phagocytosis: the process by which phagocytes surround and engulf microbes.

Prontosil: a synthetic chemical, discovered by Gerhard Domagk in the 1930s, that kills germs in the body. It was the first of the sulfanomide drugs.

Salvarsan: a chemical, discovered by Paul Ehrlich in 1909, that kills syphilis germs without injuring the host cells of the body; often referred to as Ehrlich's "magic bullet."

semisynthetic drugs: drugs, such as modern strains of penicillin, that are a combination of natural substances and artificially made chemicals.

septic wound: a wound that is infected or poisoned by invading germs.

serum: a fluid usually obtained from the blood of an immune animal or person and injected into another person to prevent or cure disease.

solvent: a substance, usually a liquid, that can dissolve other substances.

spore: a tiny cell produced by nonflowering plants, such as molds, that act like a seed and can produce a new plant.

strain: a particular variety or group of microbes or other microorganisms that share a common ancestry.

streptococcus: a particular kind of round or oval bacterium, some strains of which cause disease.

tissue: a collection of similar cells that form a part of the body and perform a common function.

vaccine: a preparation of dead or weakened bacteria or virus used to inoculate a person to prevent disease.

virus: protein-based, disease-producing agents, smaller than bacteria, that attack living tissues. Viruses cause polio, rabies, and the common cold.

FURTHER READING

Books About Alexander Fleming:

Bullock, W. A. C. *The Man Who Discovered Penicillin: The Life of Sir Alexander Fleming.* London: Faber & Faber, 1963. A brief, rather derivative biography.

Greene, Jay E., editor. *100 Great Scientists.* New York: Washington Square Press, 1964, paper. This useful reference book contains short biographies of great scientists from Hippocrates to J. D. Watson. Along with a brief account of Fleming's life are such related figures as Louis Pasteur, Joseph Lister, Dmitri Mendeleev, and Paul Ehrlich.

Hughes, W. Howard. *Alexander Fleming and Penicillin.* New York: Crane-Russak, 1977. A biography written for young adults.

Ludovici, L. J. *Fleming: Discoverer of Penicillin.* London: Andrew Dakers, 1952. This was the first published biography of Fleming. Its main interest lies in the fact that the author had direct access to his subject.

Macfarlane, Gwyn. *Alexander Fleming: The Man and the Myth.* Cambridge: Harvard University Press, 1984. This is the single best book on Fleming and a good corrective to the myth making and misinformation of earlier biographies. The author is himself a scientist, which gives him invaluable insights into each discovery. Yet the book is not overly technical and is a good read.

Maurois, André. *The Life of Sir Alexander Fleming,* translated by Gerard Hopkins. New York: E. P. Dutton, 1959. This is the standard biography by the distinguished French author. Published only four years after Fleming's death, it suffers from the kind of hero worship Maurois was known for. Nevertheless, it is finely written and is particularly good on Fleming's private life. The closing chapters on his relationship with his second wife are especially moving. Lady Amalia Fleming chose Maurois to write this "authorized" biography.

Reader's Digest. *Great Events of the 20th Century.* Pleasantville, NY: Reader's Digest Association, 1977. Another excellent historical reference book from this publisher that has a brief but well-written chapter on Fleming's discovery of penicillin. It includes a concise update on penicillin since Fleming's death.

Rowland, John. *The Penicillin Man: The Story of Sir Alexander Fleming.* New York: Roy Publishers, n.d. A young adult biograpy that is competently written but marred by a condescending tone and some glaring errors, such as the dating of Fleming's first marriage seven years after it actually happened!

Books About Other Important People and Places in the Story of Penicillin:

Colebrook, Leonard. *Almroth Wright.* London: Heinemann, 1954. A biography of Fleming's mentor and teacher by another medical colleague at St. Mary's who worked with them both.

Cope, Sir Zachary. *The History of St. Mary's Hospital Medical School.* London: Heinemann, 1954. The story of the medical school where Fleming spent his entire career, by a surgeon who also practiced there.

Macfarlane, Gwyn. *Howard Florey: The Making of a Great Scientist.* Oxford, England: Oxford University Press, 1979. An excellent biography of the man who helped purifiy penicillin and shared the Nobel Prize with Fleming.

Books About Penicillin:

Jacobs, Francine. *Breakthrough: The True Story of Penicillin.* New York: Putnam, 1985. A concise retelling of penicillin's discovery and development.

Sheehan, John C. *The Enchanted Ring: The Untold Story of Penicillin.* Cambridge, MA: MIT Press, 1982. A more thorough study of penicillin's progress to the present, by the American who developed semisynthetic penicillins.

Wilson, David. *In Search of Penicillin*. New York: Knopf, 1976. Another informative study of the "wonder drug."

INDEX